Preparing for the 2019
California Clinical Social Work
Law & Ethics Exam

Preparing for the 2019 California Clinical Social Work Law & Ethics Exam

Benjamin E. Caldwell, PsyD

Copyright © 2019 by Benjamin E. Caldwell. All rights reserved. Except as permitted under the United States Copyright Act of 1976, no portion of this publication may be reproduced or redistributed in any manner whatsoever without the prior written permission of the publisher.

First Printing: 2019

ISBN-13: 978-0-9989285-4-8

Ben Caldwell Labs
6222 Wilshire Blvd, Suite 200
Los Angeles, CA 90048

www.bencaldwelllabs.com

Ordering Information:

Discounts are available on quantity purchases by educators, corporations, associations, and others. For details, contact the publisher at the above listed address.

U.S. trade bookstores and wholesalers: Please contact Ben Caldwell Labs, 323-246-8823, or email support@bencaldwelllabs.com.

To you
You've got this
Pass

Contents

Introduction 15

What you need to know 33

Sample Questions: Answers and Rationales 113

Batting Practice 133

Practice Test Information 153

Answer Sheets 157

Practice Test 161

Practice Test: Answers and Rationales 201

Appendix: Exam Plan with Index 279

Notes 299

Acknowledgements

Deep and profound thanks to Emma Jaegle and Jeff Liebert, my teammates here at Ben Caldwell Labs, without whom this book would not exist.

Thanks to all of you who used and provided feedback on the prior generation of this book. Your feedback found its way in here.

And finally, thanks to my wife and family for their unwavering support and encouragement. We know this exam is one small step on your journey, and we want you to be successful *every* step of the way, so we created this book in hopes of making this step a bit easier. That my family understands and adopts that same mission means the world to me.

About the author

Benjamin E. Caldwell, PsyD is an Adjunct Professor teaching Law and Ethics for California State University Northridge in Los Angeles and The Wright Institute in Berkeley, CA. His research papers have been published in the *Journal of Marital and Family Therapy, American Journal of Family Therapy, Journal of Divorce and Remarriage, Journal of Systemic Therapy*, and elsewhere. He regularly gives presentations around the country on legal and ethical issues impacting therapy work. Dr. Caldwell is a California Licensed Marriage and Family Therapist (#42723).

Other books by Benjamin Caldwell:

Basics of California Law for LCSWs, LPCCs, and LCSWs, sixth edition (2019)

Preparing for the 2019 California MFT Law and Ethics Exam (2019)

Saving Psychotherapy: How therapists can bring the talking cure back from the brink (2015)

Disclaimers

Neither this book, nor any book or test preparation program, can guarantee success on an exam. Of course, your success on the test depends on your ability to learn and recall key information, and apply it in the test setting.

The information in this book is believed to be accurate at the time of printing. However, mistakes can happen, and legal and ethical standards can change quickly. It is the responsibility of each individual therapist to make sure they are remaining current with legal and ethical standards of practice.

Finally, while this book discusses legal requirements for the practice of clinical social work, it is intended to be used exclusively in the study process for the California Clinical Social Work Law and Ethics exam administered by the Board of Behavioral Sciences. Defensible multiple-choice questions are often, by necessity, much less complex than real clinical situations. **No part of this book should be construed as legal advice or as a substitute for consultation with a qualified attorney.** If you are in need of legal guidance, your professional liability insurer and your professional association may provide legal resources to you at no cost.

Introduction

First thing's first: You've got this.

The California Clinical Social Work Law and Ethics Exam is 75 questions over 90 minutes, and it is *absolutely* a test that you can pass. You've taken a graduate-level course in Law and Ethics that was probably pretty good, and probably not all that long ago. You already know a lot of this stuff! But even if your course was a while back or a bit lacking in quality, you can catch up with the current standards fairly quickly.

As licensing exams go, this exam is pretty specific. Later, when it comes time to take the ASWB Clinical Exam, you'll need to know the theory and interventions involved in many different models of treatment, you'll need to know crisis intervention, and you'll need to know a wide variety of additional information on effective clinical care *in addition to* knowing the legal and ethical rules governing the profession. But **this first test is just about those legal and ethical rules.** In that way, it's actually a better test all around: It's shorter, it's more clearly geared to public safety, and on your side, it's easier to prepare for.

You've got this.

Preparing for the 2019 California Clinical Social Work Law & Ethics Exam

About this book

This book is meant solely to help you prepare for the California Clinical Social Work Law and Ethics Exam. It aims to be as efficient as possible in providing the critical, current information you need to know to be successful on the test.
There are three main sources for this book:

1) The *NASW Code of Ethics*, available at socialworkers.org
2) *Basics of California Law for LCSWs, LPCCs, and LCSWs, sixth edition*, available on amazon.com and at bencaldwelllabs.com
3) California statutes and regulations, a summary of which is available at bbs.ca.gov (complete California law is available at leginfo.legislature.ca.gov)

In addition to those sources, a number of other articles and books were used in the development of this book, as reflected in the endnotes. This is similar to how the test itself is developed: Licensed Clinical Social Workers use source material common in the field, and develop questions assessing an examinee's knowledge of 128 "knowledge statements" outlined in the Exam Plan the BBS uses for this test.
That Exam Plan is a public document. It's available at www.bbs.ca.gov/pdf/publications/lcsw_2016-law-ethics_exam_plan.pdf for download. Because it so clearly specifies what kinds of knowledge are needed for the test, the exam plan was also key to the development of this book: **Next to each header in the study guide, you will see small numbers that start with the letter K. These numbers indicate the knowledge statements, in the BBS Exam Plan, that are addressed in that section of the Book.** As you'll see, this book covers all 128 knowledge statements necessary for the exam.
It is worth nothing that this book is not a substitute for a graduate-level Law and Ethics course, or for the textbooks used in such a course. By design, it does not explain *why* the rules governing the profession are the way that they are, nor does it aim to offer detail about how the rules can be changed. This book is not appropriate as a detailed desk reference to Cali-

fornia law for clinical practice; for that I would recommend *Basics of California Law for LCSWs, LPCCs, and LCSWs*.

This book also isn't a substitute for a larger text on ethics, or for deep understanding of the ethics codes themselves. For more detailed texts on ethical issues for CSWs, I recommend the following:

- *Ethics in Psychotherapy and Counseling* by K. S. Pope & M. J. T. Vasquez (5th edition, Wiley, 2016)
- *Issues and Ethics in the Helping Professions* by G. Corey, M. S. Corey, C. Corey, & P. Callanan (10th edition, Brooks/Cole, 2018)
- *Social Work Values and Ethics* by F. G. Reamer (5th edition, Columbia University Press, 2018)

Using this book

The study guide portion of this book is about 70 pages in total, and they're a pretty quick read. Every effort has been made to have this guide include the information you'll need for the test, and nothing more.

There are a handful of citations in the book, which refer to endnotes at the back. Those citations are used for direct quotes, longer explanations that are not critical to your understanding of material for the test, and sources other than the main sources for this book noted on the previous page.

About the Exam

Test basics

The California Clinical Social Work Law and Ethics Exam is a 75-item, 90-minute test. Of those 75 items, only 50 count toward your score. The other 25 items are being tested for possible inclusion in future test cycles. Of course, you have no way of knowing which exam items are scored and which are these experimental items, so it is in your best interest to do the best you can on every item on the test. All questions are four-option, multiple choice questions where you are tasked with choosing the *best* response from the available options.

The test is administered via computer at testing centers around the state, and can be taken at some centers outside the state as well. You can see a complete list of test centers at candidate.psiexams.com. (PSI is an independent company the BBS contracts with for the administration of their exams.) No personal items are allowed into the test centers, and they have strict rules about the clothing that examinees can wear, in order to ensure the security of testing. For example, test centers generally will not allow you to wear or bring any clothing with pockets. Some test centers have lockers where you can store personal items during your test, but some do not.

You will be seated at a workstation where your exam has been pre-loaded into the computer, and you are likely to be offered a set of earplugs or noise-cancelling headphones to use during the test if you wish. (Some examinees find these very helpful for blocking out the sound of other computers in the room, while others simply find them uncomfortable.) The PSI testing centers administer a wide variety of tests for federal and state government agencies as well as private businesses, so it is likely that the other examinees in the testing room with you will be working on several different kinds of tests. Once you've had the opportunity to get settled in and familiarize yourself with the computer you will be using, you follow the on-screen instructions to begin your exam.

Introduction

Content

Considered as a whole (but without considering experimental items), the test will break down into the following proportions:

Law – 40%
Confidentiality, privilege, and consent – 14%
Limits to confidentiality, including mandated reporting – 16%
Legal standards for professional practice – 10%

Ethics – 60%
Professional competence and preventing harm – 18%
Therapeutic relationship/services – 27%
Business practices and policies – 15%

The exam is not separated into these sections; you will get questions from these categories in fairly random order. These are merely *overall* proportions. Still, they can be helpful to know. For example, knowing that ethical issues surrounding the therapeutic relationship and services make up more than a quarter of the test, you may place an emphasis in your studying on this area.

Scoring

Your score is based on the number of non-experimental items that you answered correctly, out of 50 total. Every item is worth one point – there is no weighting of items based on difficulty, complexity, topic, or any other factor. There is also no penalty for an incorrect response; it is counted as 0 points, just the same as if the item were left blank.

The passing score on the test varies from one version of the test to the next. (Test cycles change every 90 days.) The tests given in some cycles are more challenging than others, so the BBS conducts careful statistical analysis of each test -- and of every *item* on each test -- to make sure the passing score is set appropriately. While the BBS no longer publicly announces the passing score for current test cycles, they used to. During that time, the passing score was consistently *around* 35 out of 50 scored items (70%).

Preparing for the 2019 California Clinical Social Work Law & Ethics Exam

Strategy

There are many different test-taking strategies that can help you perform well on the exam. Of course, no test-taking strategy will substitute for having detailed knowledge of the material you're being tested on. But strategies can help maximize your score by helping with items you *don't* know the answer to, and strategies can help with time and anxiety management.

In general, I defer here to your knowledge of your own strengths and challenges. You probably already know how good of a test-taker you are, and you probably already know what strategies will work best for you. (If you don't, the practice exam provided here may help you see what strategies help you the most.) Just like for studying, the only bad strategy for test-taking is one that doesn't work for you.

If you're going through a test-prep course or if you already know the strategies that help you the most, you can safely ignore the rest of this section. If not, here are three strategies specific to this exam that may help you:

1, Take the easy questions first. You can go forward and backward on the test as much as you like. Remember that you have a time limit and that items are not weighted, so a good way to start the exam (and possibly build some confidence) is to go through the whole test, marking the responses you are sure of. Then you can go back and spend more time on those items that you need more time to consider. You may find that in a very short time period, you already have half or more of the test completed – and that you are confident those answers are likely correct.

2, Use the process of elimination. Even when you aren't certain of the right response on a particular question, there is a good chance you will be able to identify one or more of the response choices as obviously *wrong*. Eliminating wrong options greatly increases your chance of getting the question right, even if you're not ultimately sure what the best answer is. One way of eliminating wrong answers is to notice when a question is asking specifically for a *legal* response or specifically for an *ethical* one – that will allow you to eliminate any responses that would fall into the other category.

The line between legal concerns and ethical concerns isn't as clear in real practice as it is on the test. The fact is, the phrase "consistent with applicable law" and equivalents appear repeatedly in the NASW code of ethics, and the (legal) unprofessional conduct category known as "general unprofessional conduct" can make ethical violations into legal ones as well. But for the purposes of the test, the two are clearly distinguished – in ways

Introduction

that can help you succeed on the test, if you understand which issues fall into which category. The table on the next page addresses where several common concerns *generally* lie: Legal, ethical, or both. There may be exceptions within each.

3, Don't get stuck in a rabbit hole. You have 90 minutes to respond to 75 questions. That gives you, on average, 72 seconds per question. If you find yourself getting hung up for more than a couple of minutes on an especially difficult question, move on. Make a mental note (or, if you're using the blank paper provided at the test center, an actual note) of the question you're struggling with and any responses you have ruled out, and then go on to other questions you may be able to answer more quickly.

4. Look for key words. Pay particular attention to items that ask specifically about ethical responsibilities or specifically about legal responsibilities. You may be able to eliminate response choices that fit into the other category. Similarly, watch for words like "must" and "should" as opposed to words like "can" or "may." Words like "must" and "should" speak to *obligations*, while words like "can" or "may" speak to *possibilities*.

5. Remember what you're being tested on. This test is specifically about your knowledge of *legal and ethical* responsibilities. It is *not* an attempt to evaluate your clinical judgment. Response choices that address *clinical* issues like treatment planning and diagnosing are likely to be distractors. In fact, it can help to push out of your mind (as much as you can) your immediate *clinical* response to a situation and focus instead on what *legal and ethical issues* the question is asking about. Some answer options may be *true but not relevant* and thus not considered correct.

6, Stay confident. You'll encounter some weird questions on the test – either things that just don't make sense to you, or items that are strangely worded. You may even see bad grammar, spelling, and sentence structure. Don't panic. These kinds of items may be the non-scored, experimental items being tested for possible inclusion as scored items on future tests. This is precisely why they do that kind of experimentation: They need to weed out bad items. It's still worth it to answer them as best you can, but if you can't figure some items out, don't let that shake your confidence in your overall knowledge. If a question is confusing, consider it *a problem with the question,* not a problem with you.

7, Go ahead and guess. Because there is no penalty for an incorrect response, if there are items you are truly unsure about, it is in your best interest to go ahead and mark your best guess. **Use the last few minutes of**

your test to mark your best guess on all remaining items you haven't already answered. The *worst* thing you can do is leave an item blank, since that gives you a 0% chance of getting the point for it. Even if you're not able to eliminate *any* of the response choices from consideration, guessing at it gives you at least a 25% chance of getting it right.

Accommodations

Accommodations are available for examinees with recognized disabilities. If you need accommodations, you will need to arrange for a letter to be sent to the BBS from your health care provider documenting your disability. Common accommodations include a quiet room for testing, or additional time to complete the exam. More information about the process of applying for accommodations, as well as the forms that must be completed, are at https://www.bbs.ca.gov/pdf/forms/specaccom.pdf

In addition to accommodations for disabilities, the BBS will also allow additional testing time for those who do not speak English as their native language. There are strict requirements to qualify for this additional time, however. The form to apply for this additional time is at https://www.bbs.ca.gov/pdf/forms/esl_specaccom.pdf

The BBS web site notes that all requests for accommodation should be received 90-120 days prior to scheduling an exam. Actual processing time varies based on time of year, application volume, staffing, and other variables.

Introduction

Legal, ethical, or both?

Legal	Both	Ethical
Informed consent for telehealth	Minors' consent for therapy	Informed consent for therapy or research
Privilege	Confidentiality	
Scope of practice		Scope of competence
Client access to records; retaining records 7 years	Maintaining records	Storage and destruction of records
Professional titles	Truth in advertising	Testimonials
Telehealth regulations	Telehealth competence	
		Monitoring impacts of personal values, attitudes and beliefs
		Countertransference
Ownership of records	Client autonomy	
	Non-discrimination	Cultural competence
Fee disclosures	Fees for referrals	Bartering
Child, elder, & dependent adult abuse reporting		
Involuntary hospitalization	Crisis management	Collaboration across systems
Insurance parity		Advocacy with payors
		Termination and non-abandonment
Providing *Professional Therapy Never Includes Sex* brochure	Sexual relationships	Multiple relationships
	Monitoring self for impairment	Assisting impaired colleagues
Licensure requirements	Supervision	

See the important cautionary notes about this chart on the previous pages. In real life, the categories aren't as cleanly divided as they are for test study purposes here.

Also, a quick reminder: Stuff like this takes a long time to put together. **Please don't share this or other content from this guide online.** Doing so violates our copyright (there's some irony in breaking the law while preparing for a law and ethics test), and ultimately drives up prices for everyone. Thanks for being awesome and not doing that. ☺

Like the rest of this book, this chart is © Copyright 2019 Ben Caldwell Labs Inc.

Preparing for the 2019 California Clinical Social Work Law & Ethics Exam

Before the test

As soon as you register as an Associate CSW

You need to take the Law & Ethics Exam in your first year of associate registration in order to renew that registration. (More on that in a moment.) But there is no need to wait until the end of that first year to take the test. In fact, **it may be advantageous to you to schedule the exam as soon as possible once you have your registration number from the state.**

Taking the test early means you will be more recently out of graduate school, and much of the information contained on the test will probably be fresher in your mind. It may be easier to prepare for the exam at this point than it would be much later, when some of the material may have been forgotten. In addition, taking the exam early in the year means the consequences of failing are minimal: You just wait 90 days and then try again, presumably studying in the meantime. If you don't take the test until the end of the registration year, failing it means having to take a 12-hour continuing education course in Law and Ethics.

If you can go into your test confident that you know the material *and* assured that failing is fairly inconsequential, you are less likely to have test anxiety stand in the way of a strong performance.

Weeks or months before

The material on which you will be tested is largely consistent with what you would have learned in graduate school, particularly what you learned in your Law and Ethics class. So a lot of your preparation will simply be re-familiarizing yourself with that material, and making sure you're caught up on any recent changes that have taken place in the legal and ethical rules governing the profession.

There are, of course, lots of ways to **study the material for the exam.** Do what you know works for you. The exam does not contain trick questions, and there is no "secret" way to study. The only wrong way to study is a way that doesn't work for you. If you work well with flash cards, make them. If you're someone who does better with reading and rereading, well, hopefully this book is helpful! The point is, trust your instincts and experience when deciding how to study, and how much. Some will find that an hour a night is all they can handle, while others will want to take several-hour-long blocks of time to study. Similarly, some find it more useful to study with friends or colleagues who are also about to test, while others prefer to study on their own.

The most important thing to do several weeks before the test is to **schedule your exam.** Review the list of test centers at candidate.psiexams.com and choose the one that is most convenient to you. While all of the test centers are designed to have ample parking and similar testing conditions, you might want to consult with others who have recently taken exams at locations close to you. They can prepare you for things like the friendliness (or lack thereof) of test center staff, which can make a big difference in your testing experience. Note that the center you choose to schedule might not be the one that is geographically closest to you; you might find there's one farther away that is easier to schedule on your preferred day and time, or in a neighborhood that you like to visit.

One thing you may find helpful once you have your test scheduled is to **clear your test day of other obligations.** Arrange to take the day off from work, and don't put any other appointments on your schedule. You will want to focus squarely on the test. And once it's over, you will not want to go back to work right away. If you pass, you'll want (and deserve!) a bit of celebration, and if you don't pass, you'll want some time to shake it off.

Another thing to address once your test is scheduled: **tell employers, supervisors, and loved ones about your upcoming test.** Part of this is simply pragmatic: They will need to know that you will be *entirely* unreachable, even in the event of an emergency, during the time you are taking the test. (Cell phones are, of course, not allowed in the testing room.) But part of it is also to shore up social support: It's good to go into a test knowing that a lot of people are cheering for you, and that they will be ready to celebrate with you once you pass.

The week before

Since you schedule your exam by phone or online, you may not be familiar with the specific location of the test center where you will take the exam. It can reduce anxiety on your test day if you actually **visit the test center** during the week before the test. Try to go to the center in advance around the same time of day that you'll be going for the actual test. This can help you get a feel for traffic, parking, and the like. Based on how long it takes you to get there, you can better plan your actual test day, making sure to give yourself ample time for unexpected delays.

The week before the test is also the time to **wrap up studying**. Hopefully by this time you're feeling confident and ready. If not, it's worth taking an honest look at *why* you're not feeling that way. Is it simple anxiety about the test, or is it a recognition that you don't know the material as well as you should? Anxiety can be managed through relaxation techniques, time with friends, and perhaps a visit to your own therapist. If there are parts of the material you are struggling with, you still have time to shore up your weak points before going in to the exam.

The wrap-up process does involve studying, of course, but **take care of yourself** during this time. There is indeed such thing as too much studying: if it is interfering with sleep, your ability to care for your clients, or your relationships with loved ones, you may find that simply adding on more study time this late in the process will do you more harm than good.

Part of taking care of yourself can be to **adopt a mantra**, or a brief statement you can use repetitively to center yourself and calm your nerves. (A mantra can be part of a larger spiritual or meditation practice, but doesn't have to be.) Here are a few you can choose from, or create one that is a good fit for you:

> *It's just a test. It doesn't define me as a person or as a therapist.*
> *I am ready.*
> *I've had good education, good supervision, and good preparation.*
> *I will be the same therapist after the test that I am before it.*
> *This is a milestone, just one checkpoint on a larger journey.*
> *I will pass.*
> *My friends and family will love me the same no matter what happens.*
> *I know the things I need to know.*

Occasionally, people find that they are really not ready for the test at this point, and may consider rescheduling it for a later date. That's fine, but before taking this step, consider whether it is truly about your readiness, or whether it simply is a reflection of anxiety creeping up on you. If it's anxiety, putting off the test may just mean you repeat the experience a few weeks later.

The day before

The day before the test, spend time reviewing what you know and making sure you have everything ready for the next day. You may want to prepare a checklist of things to do and things to bring to the test with you, such as a photo ID, paperwork confirming the test time and location, and the like. (Remember that most test centers will not allow you to bring personal items into the exam room. Some test centers have lockers you can use to store personal items during the test, but not all do.) Make sure you eat well and get a good night's sleep the night before the exam.

The day of the test

Different people have different ideas about whether it is helpful to do some last-minute studying on the actual day of the test. Again, do what works best for you. Some find that reviewing material one last time increases their confidence, as they recognize material, get practice questions right, and generally go into the test feeling good about how much they know. Others find that continuing to review at the last minute only increases their anxiety.

The most important thing you can do on the day of the test is to keep your anxiety in check. Have a normal, healthy breakfast. (Food and drinks are not allowed in the testing room, so don't go in on an empty stomach.) Get a pep talk from your partner or a close friend. If you've chosen a mantra, spend time repeating it to yourself.

Before you leave home or work for the test, make sure you have the documents you will need to get in: your photo ID and the confirmation from PSI that includes the date, time, and location of your test. Without these materials, you may not be allowed to take the exam.

After the test

Unless you have a disability accommodation that requires paper-and-pencil testing, you will find out immediately whether you passed the exam. If you pass, congratulations! You will not need to go through another test until you complete your hours of supervised experience for licensure and are sitting for the ASWB Clinical Exam.

If you do *not* pass on your first try, but there is ample time left before your registration renewal, then failing is largely inconsequential. You can take the test again after a 90-day waiting period, and pass on that attempt. (If you start early, you could attempt the test three times before your renewal comes up.)

If there isn't time to attempt again before your renewal, you can still renew your registration; the requirement for renewal is that you have *attempted* the test at least once. But once you renew your registration, when you apply to retake the exam you will need to show proof that you have completed a 12-hour CE course in California Law & Ethics for CSWs.

The BBS will not allow anyone to register with a second registration number, or to sit for the Clinical Exam, until they have passed the Law and Ethics Exam.

Additional information

If you have additional questions about the exam process or requirements, the BBS has made a great deal of information available on their web site, at www.bbs.ca.gov.

Hopefully this book will be a helpful guide to the information you will need to know for the exam. The more you can integrate the information here into your understanding of clinical work, the better off you will be. Deep knowledge of the information is, of course, likely to be the most important factor in whether you pass the test. But it isn't the only factor.

The BBS has been lukewarm toward test-prep companies, out of concern that the companies may suggest there is some "secret knowledge" behind the test when there is not. All of the information you need to know for the exam comes from common materials in the field, including the NASW code of ethics (freely available online), state law and regulation (also freely available online), and the same law and ethics textbooks commonly used in graduate courses in the state.

Preparing for the 2019 California Clinical Social Work Law & Ethics Exam

Here we go!

The next section is a summary of information likely to be included on the exam. While the BBS uses 128 knowledge statements, they've been organized here in such a way that should make them easier to study and retain. I've kept the descriptions as brief and simple as possible.

I've divided the next section into seven subsections:

- Parameters of practice
- Documentation & disclosures
- Confidentiality & privilege
- Treatment
- The business of clinical social work ✻
- Non-therapist roles
- Unprofessional conduct

You can see that some of these correspond with the categories used when considering how the test itself breaks down into different proportions. Given the number of questions about treatment you are likely to encounter, some additional time in that subsection may be warranted.

If you have questions about any of the explanations here, or want to dive deeper on any of the subjects covered in this book, you best first stop is the primary source material used in the development of this book.
You've got this.
Good luck!

What you need to know

Parameters of practice

This section covers the larger boundaries of therapy: What can you do as a CSW, and whom can you treat? What steps are necessary when your personal values or beliefs are getting in the way of quality care? And what are some of the overriding principles of ethical and effective psychotherapy?

Scope of practice K34

Your scope of practice is set in state law. It specifies what someone with an LCSW license can legally do. Now, California's CSW scope of practice language is long and a bit obtuse.[1] So rather than quote the whole thing, we'll just talk *about* it.

The CSW scope of practice allows you to work with individuals, couples, families, and groups. (Throughout this book, when you see the word "client," it may refer to an individual, couple, or family.) The CSW scope of practice specifically allows you to use "counseling and [...] applied psychotherapy," making you a psychotherapist. And it allows you to use the training you received in your required coursework – which is key to understanding that CSWs can independently diagnose mental illness.

One of the most important pieces in understanding scope of practice is understanding its limits. **CSWs *cannot* provide legal advice, medical advice, or other forms of guidance that are outside the CSW scope of practice.** Recommending that a client take a certain medication, for example, would be outside of the CSW scope of practice.

Whether CSWs can use psychological tests in has been more questionable. Nothing in state law appears to prohibit CSWs from using psychological tests. A 1984 attorney general opinion clarified that *MFTs* can use psychological tests under two conditions: It has to be with clients the MFT is seeing for therapy, and the MFT must have to have adequate training in administering the test. It is not clear, however, whether this opinion would apply to CSWs, particularly considering that the laws governing MFTs require that they take coursework in psychological testing while CSWs have no similar requirement. It is certainly safe to say, though, that a CSW who does not have training in psychological assessment instruments should not be using those instruments.

It is helpful here to understand the difference between scope of *practice* – which is set in state law, and is the same for every CSW in the state – and scope of *competence*, which is based on your specific education, training, and experience. Scope of competence varies by individual CSW, and is primarily an ethical issue. It is discussed later, in the Treatment section.

Self-awareness K46-48, 50-51

Impairments. Good social workers are keenly aware of their own limitations. If you are struggling with a serious emotional problem, mental or physical illness, or substance use, it can interfere with your ability to provide effective therapy. In addition, if you have a strong emotional reaction to a particular client – perhaps because their struggle mirrors one you have gone through, or because there is something in the client's behavior that you strongly dislike – you may not be able to provide effective services.

Responding to impairments. CSWs need to know the referrals and resources available in the event that the therapist is struggling with an impairment and needs to step away from client care, either temporarily or on a longer-term basis. (Knowledge of appropriate referrals and resources comes up multiple times in the BBS Exam Plan, as it is important in many different sets of circumstances. Obviously, the test will not ask what the closest hospital is, since the same test is being given across the state. But you may be asked about the *kinds* of referrals and resources that would be most appropriate to a given situation. Referrals should always be appropriate to the level and type of client need.)

For the therapist, obviously seeking treatment is appropriate when the problem is a serious emotional problem, mental or physical illness, or substance use. If the issue is a strong reaction to the client, the CSW should seek supervision and consultation, and consider going to therapy. In whatever time it takes for the CSW to resolve their impairment, protecting the welfare of the client is the highest priority.

Methods to facilitate transfer. In some cases, the impairment of a CSW will lead to their needing to transfer clients to other therapists. If it is possible and appropriate, the CSW may have a termination session with the client, focused on transitioning them to a new provider. The CSW should provide appropriate referrals based on client need. The CSW and client should consider a Release of Information authorizing the transfer of client records to the new provider, and authorizing the old and new therapists to communicate to ensure continuity of care. The CSW should follow up with the new provider to transfer the records and coordinate care appropriately.

Personal values, attitudes, and beliefs. CSWs are ethically prohibited from influencing client decisions on preferred treatment or outcomes based on personal values, attitudes, and beliefs. (Going forward, I'll just say "attitudes" to refer collectively to "values, attitudes, and beliefs.") Obviously, it is important for CSWs to be aware of their own attitudes and how they might impact the therapy process. Social workers allowing for their attitudes to influence them might pathologize the behavior of clients the social worker doesn't like, leading to incorrect diagnoses and poor treatment decisions. They might show bias toward one or more family members, impacting the effectiveness of couple or family work. They might become overly friendly (or overly hostile) with a client. They might place their own belief about a particular problem above current scientific knowledge in the field. Ultimately, the social worker is likely to miss or misinterpret important clinical information, decreasing the likelihood of effective therapy.

Managing the impact of therapist attitudes. So what happens, then, when a CSW becomes aware that they have personal attitudes that are entering into the therapy room? It depends on the nature of what is arising. If the therapist is experiencing judgment or bias toward the client based on personal attitudes, the therapist should carefully consider how those attitudes are impacting treatment. The therapist may seek out supervision or consultation to ensure quality of care, and may go to their own therapy to identify the source of the attitude, working to change it if appropriate. If the therapist attitude is likely to continue interfering in the therapeutic relationship, the therapist may consider referring the client to another therapist – but must be cautious to avoid client abandonment, and to ensure that the referral is not discriminatory in nature. If the therapist refers clients out based on personal attitudes about race, gender, or other protected characteristics, the therapist may be engaging in discrimination.

Preparing for the 2019 California Clinical Social Work Law & Ethics Exam

Client autonomy K62, 86-88

Client autonomy in treatment decisions. Clients have the fundamental right to choose for themselves what kinds of mental health and social services they will participate in. There are exceptions to this, such as for clients who present an imminent danger to themselves or others and thus can be involuntarily hospitalized. Generally speaking, though, clients can choose their treatment type, treatment provider, and treatment goals as they see fit. (Some goals would be considered inappropriate for therapy, such as a parent bringing their child into therapy in hopes of changing the child's sexual orientation. While a parent is certainly free to pursue this goal, it would not be appropriate for a therapist to attempt to offer this treatment.) Consistent with this principle, clients can also discontinue treatment or change treatment provider at any time.

When a social worker is working with a client who lacks decision-making capacity, the CSW is ethically obligated to take reasonable steps to safeguard that client's interests and rights.

Collaborative relationship between client and therapist. It is the role of the CSW to *assist* clients in making important life decisions, not to make those decisions for the client. The NASW Code of Ethics requires CSWs to respect clients' right to make decisions on their own, such as decisions about entering or leaving a relationship, with the CSW assisting clients in their efforts to identify and clarify goals. In your role as a CSW, you help clients to understand the consequences of various decisions they may be considering, and whether those decisions are likely to bring the client closer to the goals they would like to achieve. But the ultimate decision-making is up to the client.

This sometimes gets misunderstood as a ban on advice-giving. Many CSWs directly advise their clients, and this can be consistent with models of psychotherapy that place the therapist in a directive, expert role. Even the assigning of homework, which is a common intervention in many therapeutic models, can be considered giving advice, and it is certainly acceptable to suggest that clients try out specific new skills in the week ahead.

Methods to assist client decision-making. There are many ways a CSW can assist a client in decision-making and clarifying goals without interfering with the client's autonomy in making those decisions. The therapist can help the client list various courses of action they could take in a difficult time, often expanding the possibilities beyond those the client may see on their own. The therapist can help the client foresee possible consequences of each of the possible courses of action, using current research as well as the therapist's knowledge of the client's specific context. The therapist can assess the client's readiness to act. The therapist can reflect and validate the client's excitement about some possibilities and anxiety about others. Each of these tasks facilitates the client making an important decision on their own, with the therapist's guidance and support.

Best interests of the client K79-81

How legal and ethical obligations impact therapy. Our legal and ethical obligations exist primarily to protect the best interests of clients. They can have the side effect of protecting therapists, by setting clear standards of professional behavior (and thus protecting us from accusations of being unprofessional when we are not), but they fundamentally exist to protect clients *from* us.

Sometimes, our legal and ethical obligations can create an inconvenience for therapist and client alike. Clients may not read every word of a long informed consent document, and therapists may not want to spend time in therapy discussing the limits of confidentiality. However, failing to meet our obligations can place clients at risk in a variety of ways. We fulfill these obligations because it is good for clients, even when it isn't convenient.

Social workers are instructed in multiple ways through the NASW Code of Ethics to inform clients when legal and ethical standards of the profession will limit the client's rights or change the therapist's role. For example, the ethics code requires that CSWs advise clients of those instances (such as child abuse reporting) where the therapist's responsibility to the larger society supersedes the therapist's responsibility to the client.

Conflicts between legal and ethical obligations. There are many times when there is not a direct conflict between law and ethics, but they set different standards. For example, the law may offer a stricter standard than the ethics codes, or vice versa. In these instances, a CSW should follow the stricter standard, regardless of which set of rules it comes from.

If there is a direct conflict between the code of ethics and the law – that is, if the law says that you *must* do one thing, while the code of ethics says that you *must* do something that is different from and incompatible with what the law requires – the law wins. CSWs should follow the law, and practice in accordance with the code of ethics to the greatest extent possible.

Conflicts between agency and ethical obligations. It is also common for CSWs to work in settings where ethics codes conflict with workplace policy. The NASW code requires CSWs to make their commitment to ethical standards known to the organization, and to take reasonable steps to resolve the issue in a way that allows the social worker to practice in keeping with their ethical responsibilities. Social work administrators have an additional ethical responsibility to work within their roles to change any policies that might conflict with, or otherwise discourage compliance with, the ethics code. The overriding principle is clear: Agency policy does not provide an excuse for CSWs to ignore their ethical duties.

Consultation and collaboration K43, 66-68, 72, 89-90

Collaborating with other professionals. Social workers are not just encouraged but *expected* to participate in interdisciplinary teams and to establish collaborative professional relationships to further the welfare of the client. Establishing collegial relationships can be as simple as friendly outreach. Sometimes it requires multiple efforts, or proof that your client has authorized you to discuss their case. CSWs are expected to help clearly establish the professional and ethical obligations of each individual member of a treatment team.

Once your role on a treatment team has been clearly established, you are expected to contribute to the team's work in order to support the client. CSWs are ethically expected to "participate in and contribute to decisions that affect the well-being of clients by drawing on the perspectives, values, and experiences of the social work profession."[2] This, of course, requires that the CSW be familiar with those current professional perspectives, values, and experiences.

Occasionally, a decision made by a treatment team will raise ethical concerns for a CSW. In those instances, the CSW should try to resolve the issue through appropriate channels. If that fails, the CSW should seek out additional means of addressing their concerns to support the client. This doesn't mean that the CSW should use *in*appropriate means to resolve the issue, but rather that the first option is always to try to resolve the issue directly with the team. If that doesn't work, then the CSW may make use of other systems to support the client as well as possible.

Protecting client rights in consultation and collaboration. Of course, CSWs are encouraged to regularly consult with other professionals and community resources to promote quality client care. It is common for CSWs to collaborate and consult with physicians, teachers, social service providers, and other important persons in a client's life. CSWs are expected to be aware of colleagues' competence and expertise, so that when consulting is appropriate, the CSW can easily find a knowledgeable person. Ethically, the CSW should only seek consult from someone with appropriate knowledge or competence.

When doing such consultations, CSWs respect the confidentiality of their clients. Each member of the treatment unit must give their permission for clinical information to be shared with any outsider, unless an exception to confidentiality applies (see later discussion for more on this). Even where permission has been given, the CSW should disclose the minimum amount of confidential information necessary to fulfill the purpose of the consultation.

Effects of concurrent treatment. When done well, concurrent treatment can maximize therapeutic gains. Coordinated care among multiple therapists can mean that family members receive individual therapy to work on their individual concerns at the same time they are receiving family therapy to address relational issues. This may speed improvement by addressing multiple levels of concern at once, and by reducing the homeostatic processes in family systems that can keep individual symptoms locked in place.

Concurrent treatment can also cause problems, however, especially when the multiple therapists involved are not in communication with one another. It is not in the best interests of clients to go to one therapist who encourages the client to create distance from the client's mother, and then to go to another therapist who is working to develop a closer relationship between mother and client.

Ethical guidelines for concurrent psychotherapy. Clients are likely to be involved in multiple systems of care at the same time. A client may have a physician prescribing medication, an individual therapist, and a CSW providing family treatment, all at once. This can create problems for the client if the different treatment providers are pursuing different goals or are not communicating with one another.

Social workers are specifically instructed to consider carefully what the client's needs are before agreeing to work with them, if the client is also receiving services from another agency or therapist. You should discuss the nature of the existing relationship, the risks and benefits of entering into a new therapy process, and any other important implications. This serves the purpose of ensuring coordinated care. You also should discuss whether it would be in the client's interests to have them sign a release of information allowing you to consult with the other service provider.

Diversity and nondiscrimination K82-85

Ethical standards for non-discrimination. The NASW code of ethics states that social workers shall not "practice, condone, facilitate, or collaborate with any form of discrimination" in professional services based on the following factors:

- Race
- Ethnicity
- National origin
- Color
- Sex
- Sexual orientation
- Gender identity or expression
- Age
- Marital status
- Political belief
- Religion

- Immigration status
- Mental or physical ability

Diversity factors in therapy. Social workers are specifically called upon to recognize the strengths that exist in all cultures, and to work toward reducing discrimination and exploitation on societal levels. CSWs understand the impact of culture on human behavior. This can mean, for example, recognizing when a behavior is culturally appropriate and thus should not be diagnosed as a mental illness, even if it otherwise meets diagnostic criteria.

Virtually any area of difference between client and therapist has the potential to impact the therapy process. While discussions of diversity in the US tend to center on issues of race, ethnicity, and (more recently) sexual orientation, a wide variety of other factors can impact a client's identity and cultural norms. In addition to all of the factors listed in the non-discrimination standards above, therapy can be impacted by differences between client and therapist in urban versus rural setting, educational level, regional identity, and many more.

Ethical standards for providing services to diverse groups. Social workers are ethically obligated to be mindful of all forms of historical and social prejudice, as this prejudice can lead to misdiagnosing clients or pathologizing culturally-accepted behavior. In addition, CSWs "obtain education about and seek to understand the nature of social diversity and oppression with respect to" all of the factors listed in the non-discrimination standard.[3] Social workers should be able to demonstrate competence in providing services that are sensitive to client culture and to cultural differences.

Physical contact. Touch in therapy, from a handshake to holding a client while they cry, can be a powerful part of the therapeutic bond. However, touch also risks being misunderstood as romantic or sexual in nature. Depend on the therapist, the client, and the setting, physical touch may or may not be culturally and professionally appropriate. CSWs who touch their clients should set and abide by appropriate, clear, and culturally sensitive boundaries on physical contact during service delivery.

Improving knowledge, skills, awareness, and sensitivity. So what can a therapist do when approached by a client who is different from the therapist in ways that impact the therapy process? While postmodern models of therapy encourage CSWs to allow clients to inform the therapist about the client's life and circumstances, it is likely to be inadequate for a therapist to take no other action to improve their knowledge and skills around the relevant diversity issues. The social worker could:

- Attend a continuing education training on working with the client's population
- Seek consultation or supervision from other therapists who identify as part of, or regularly work with, the client's population
- Seek out greater exposure to the client's population
- Read articles and other literature on the client's population
- Attend their own therapy to address issues of bias

What You Need to Know

Sample Questions *See page 114 for answers and rationales*

1. A client sees an LCSW at a local community clinic for court-mandated anger management groups. The client comes to dislike the LCSW and becomes disruptive, frequently comparing the group to jail, and saying "I'm not free when I'm here." In considering her ethical responsibilities, the LCSW should:

   a. Empathize and validate the client's feeling of disempowerment.
   b. Terminate therapy with the client and refer them back to court.
   c. Remind the client that he is free to attend any anger management group he wishes, or none at all.
   d. Threaten to inform the court of his statements if he continues, and encourage him to become more open to the group process.

2. A 14-year-old client consented to her own treatment at a nonprofit agency, which agreed to treat her for $5/session. The client tells the therapist (an LCSW) that the client has been abusing a friend's prescription painkillers. Legally, the LCSW should:

   a. Notify the local child protective service agency.
   b. Notify the client's parent or guardian, as the behavior is considered high-risk.
   c. Work with the client to develop a plan to gradually reduce dosage and ultimately stop the client's drug use.
   d. Document the discussion and refer the client to a physician.

Documentation & disclosures

What we tell clients about therapy is often just as important as the therapy itself. Many of our legal and ethical requirements relate directly to the information given to clients about the therapy process, and the records we keep of the therapy process.

Informed Consent & Disclosures K7, 36, 60-65

Informed consent. In order for a client to offer consent that is truly *informed*, they need a reasonable amount of *information* about the treatment process. CSWs have an ethical responsibility to provide clients with appropriate information about the treatment process, so that the client can make an informed decision about whether they want to participate. Because treatment plans and methods can change during therapy, informed consent for treatment is best understood not as a single event but as an ongoing process.

Social workers obtain consent before searching for information about a client online, unless there is an imminent danger or other "compelling professional reason."

Facilitating client decisions about treatment. The NASW code of ethics requires CSWs to provide enough information to clients that the clients can make meaningful choices about whether to start therapy. The nature of this information may vary by therapist and by treatment type. CSWs are ethically obligated to inform clients of:

- The purpose of the services being provided
- Risks related to those services
- Limits on services due to requirements of third-party payers
- Costs
- Alternatives

- The client's right to refuse or withdraw consent
- Limitations and risks of electronic treatment, if applicable
- The time frame covered by the consent

Clients should be given the opportunity to ask questions about informed consent. If the client is receiving services involuntarily (as happens with court-mandated clients, as one example), they still should be informed about the issues above, and the extent of their right to refuse service. Specific consent should be obtained for any third-party observation or for any audio or video recording of services.

All of this information must be given in clear and understandable language. If a client is not literate, the therapist should provide a detailed verbal explanation, and document that they have done so. If the client does not easily understand the language being used for informed consent (for example, a client primarily speaks Spanish and is attending therapy with a CSW who delivers informed consent documents in English), the therapist should take appropriate steps to make sure the client can understand what they are agreeing to. This may involve bringing in an interpreter.

Client right to self-determination. Clients have a fundamental right to self-determination (also commonly referred to as autonomy), meaning that they alone can choose whether to participate in treatment, what the goals of treatment should be, and what provider to use. (Some therapy goals might be outside of the CSW's scope of practice or competence, or otherwise inappropriate for therapy. The client remains free to pursue those goals, but the CSW could not provide services to assist the clients toward reaching those goals.)

Even when treatment is taking place by court order, clients typically are able to choose their provider. CSWs respect clients' rights to choose whether to start therapy and whether to leave it at any time. One of the critical components of informed consent is ensuring that clients are aware of their ability to make their own decisions regarding treatment.

Culturally and developmentally appropriate methods. CSWs should gain consent for treatment in a manner that is culturally and developmentally appropriate. If a client is illiterate, does not read English, or is otherwise unable to make sense of the informed consent document, their signature on it would not truly reflect informed consent. The informed consent process would be better served with a verbal discussion in language that the client can understand, followed by careful documentation in the client's record that this conversation had occurred. CSWs also should be aware of the possibility that clients may be attending therapy against their wishes, at the demand of a family member or others; in such instances, it is important for the CSW to determine whether the client is truly providing voluntary consent for treatment. (Mandated clients, who are different from those who would simply prefer to not be in therapy, are discussed separately below.)

Clients who can't provide voluntary consent. When a client is unable to provide voluntary consent for treatment, the CSW remains responsible for protecting client welfare. Clients may be unable to voluntarily consent for treatment if they are under the influence of drugs or alcohol, if they have been involuntarily hospitalized as a danger to themselves or others, or if they are a child brought to treatment by their parents, as a few examples.

In these instances, the CSW would still take steps to promote client welfare and facilitate the client's ability to make decisions about treatment to the degree possible. In the case of a client under the influence of drugs or alcohol, the CSW may simply take steps to keep the client safe until the influence of the drug has worn off and the client can voluntarily consent to further treatment. A more thorough informed consent process may take place at that point. If a client has been involuntarily hospitalized, the CSW may remind them of their remaining rights. In the case of a minor, a CSW may utilize an *assent* agreement, which spells out the purpose, risks, and benefits of therapy in a way that is developmentally appropriate to the child, and allows them to ask questions about the therapy. An assent agreement may not be legally enforceable (in other words, it is not the same as legal consent for treatment, which may need to be signed by a parent), but still serves to show that you met your ethical responsibility to provide an informed consent process appropriate to the client.

Even when a client is mandated for treatment, they may retain more control over that treatment than they believe, and consent can still in some ways be considered voluntary. Generally speaking, clients mandated to treatment by a court or other outside entity retain their right to choose their treatment provider. They may be required by a court to be in therapy, but typically, they don't have to be in therapy *with you*. CSWs working with mandated clients should clarify the CSW's role and the limits of confidentiality that will apply to the mandated services. This clarification helps protect client rights, as they can choose whether to go forward in treatment under those rules. Of course, refusing treatment entirely may have negative consequences for a mandated client, but they are still free to make that choice.

Treatment of minors. In most cases, parents provide consent for the treatment of their child. Anyone under age 18 is a minor under state law, and parents can consent for treatment on their child's behalf. If a minor has two legal parents, then typically either parent can provide consent for therapy for the minor.

If the minor's parents are divorced, consent becomes more complicated. The CSW should request a copy of the custody order to determine which parent's consent is necessary for treatment of the minor. In joint custody, typically either parent can provide consent on their own. If one parent has sole custody, only that parent can provide consent for the minor's treatment. If they refuse or withdraw their consent, the CSW should not treat the minor.[4]

Other caregivers may sometimes bring a minor in for therapy. Another relative who lives in the same home as the minor may provide consent for the minor's treatment if they sign a "Caregiver's Authorization Affidavit." The necessary language of this document is specified in state law.

Minors as young as 12 may be seen *without* parental consent if the minor is mature enough to participate intelligently in treatment. That determination is made by the therapist. In these cases, the therapist still must either make an effort to contact the child's parents, or document why they believe doing so would be harmful. Parents do not have a right to access records for their child if the child consented independently, and parents cannot be forced to pay for services provided to their child without the parents' consent.

Guardians and representatives. When clients are unable to make informed decisions on their own, their guardians and legal representatives have the right and responsibility to make choices on the client's behalf. Most commonly, this happens when a parent or legal guardian consents to the treatment of a minor. However, it can also apply when a client under conservatorship is put into treatment by their conservator, or when a court-appointed *guardian ad litem* seeks treatment for minors involved in a custody dispute. In these and other instances, guardians and legal representatives are responsible for making informed decisions about treatment that will be in the best interest of the client.

Disclosing fees. Under state law, you must inform clients before treatment begins of (1) the fee they will be charged and (2) the basis upon which that fee was computed. If you're confused about that second part, think about the sliding-fee scales used at many training clinics: *Client income* is the basis on which the fee is computed. As another example, some CSWs charge more for couple or family sessions than they do for individual sessions. Others may charge specific fees for appearing in court on the client's behalf. Those are both fine, but clients need to know about this before treatment starts. Failure to disclose fees and their basis prior to starting treatment is considered unprofessional conduct.

Documentation K8-13 (except "delivery" in K12), 105-108

Documentation of services. Documentation of therapy is both a legal and ethical requirement. Neither state law nor professional ethics define the specific *content* that needs to be in treatment records, and there are a wide variety of formats for things like assessments and progress notes. However, all CSWs are legally required to keep records that are consistent with "sound clinical judgment, the standards of the profession, and the nature of the services being rendered."[5] As we will see, there are some specific things that legally must be documented when they occur, such as consent for telehealth services.

Professional ethics demand that treatment records be accurate and reflect the services provided. Documentation should also be completed in a timely manner to ensure continuity of care. When a CSW is suddenly unavailable, due to illness or any other reason, accurate and up-to-date records ensure that clients can be adequately cared for until the CSW is able to return.

The NASW Code of Ethics *specifically* demands that CSWs document the following:

- Informed consent for evaluation or research
- Client requests for records and, where applicable, reasons for refusing access to part or all of those records

Many other elements of documentation can be reasonably inferred from the code, even though they are not stated outright. For example, the code requires that CSWs *obtain* informed consent for therapy. While this consent does not specifically need to be in writing (and indeed, there are times when a written informed consent document may be inadequate, such as when the client cannot read or understand the language the document is written in), it is reasonable to assume that consent should be documented in some form.

The NASW code also addresses information that does *not* belong in a client's record. Documentation should only include information that is directly relevant to the services being provided. This helps to protect the privacy of clients.

Protecting the confidentiality of records. CSWs should protect the confidentiality of client records while services are being delivered and after the services have been completed. Methods for protecting the confidentiality of records include:

- Keeping paper records in a secure, locked file cabinet
- Keeping electronic records in a secure, encrypted format
- Carefully controlling who has access to client files
- Shredding paper files to dispose of them

Maintenance of records. Under state law, records must be maintained for at least 7 years following the last professional contact. If you are working with a minor, records must be maintained for at least 7 years after the minor turns 18. The NASW Code of Ethics reinforces this legal standard.

CSWs have an ethical responsibility to store records in ways that allow reasonable future access to them. At the same time, you should take reasonable steps to ensure they remain secure and confidential. When the time comes that you dispose of old client records, this disposal should also be done in a manner that protects security and confidentiality. A CSW should never simply throw old client files in the trash.

Client access to records. Clients generally have a legal and ethical right to access their records, though there are some limitations on this. Unless you believe that the release of records to the client would be harmful, you must comply with their request in a timely manner: Within 5 days if the client simply wants to inspect their records, and within 15 days if the client wants a copy of their record. You cannot refuse a client's request for records simply because they owe you money. You can, however, charge for reasonable costs associated with accessing and copying the client's file, and you can provide a summary of the file rather than the full record if you prefer (this typically must be within 10 days of the client's request). Any client who inspects their record and believes some part of it to be incomplete or incorrect can submit a brief statement to be included in the client file.

If you believe that releasing records to a client would be harmful to them, you may refuse to do so. If you refuse, you need to document the request and your reason for refusal. Under California law, the client may then request that a third-party professional review the records to see whether that third party agrees with you that the record should not be released.

Couple, family, and group treatment present challenges when one client requests records but the others involved in treatment are either unaware of the request or do not agree to it. The NASW Code of Ethics requires CSWs to seek clarity, as early as possible, about policies for confidentiality from all participants in couple, family, or group therapy.

When clients are given access to records that identify or discuss other individuals, the CSW should act to protect the confidentiality of those other individuals. This may involve releasing a treatment summary as described above, or by redacting portions of the record that are not directly relevant to the person requesting records.

Because clients are typically not trained mental health professionals, it may be easy for them to misunderstand or misinterpret the information contained in their records. CSWs can minimize this risk by using clear language in their documentation, going through the record with the client upon release, explaining diagnoses and other clinical decisions, and providing the client the opportunity to ask questions about their records if they wish.

Release of records to others. Records of treatment can be released to third parties if the client requests it or if there is some other appropriate legal authorization. Most commonly, clients request that their records be forwarded to another therapist or health care provider for continuity of care, or they request that records be provided to their insurance company for the purpose of receiving reimbursement.

When a client requests that their records be released to a third party, this request typically must be in writing, and it must be signed and dated by the client or their legal representative.

There are some instances when a specific authorization to release information is *not* required by law, such as when the information is needed by another provider or health care facility to for the purposes of diagnosis or treatment (in an emergency, for example, there may not be time to gather written authorization), or when the information is required as part of a billing process.

Records are also sometimes released by court order, which is its own form of legal authorization. Subpoenas and court orders are discussed further in the section on Confidentiality & Privilege.

Emergency disclosures of confidential information may be necessary if the client poses an immediate risk of harm to themselves or others. In such instances, both state law and professional ethics allow for the release of information that would otherwise be confidential. However, the information released should be the *minimum* amount of information necessary to achieve the purposes of the disclosure. For example, if you are sending paramedics to a client who has called you expressing active and immediate suicidality, the paramedics likely need to know the client's appearance, location, and state of mind. Specific circumstances would determine whether the disclosure of any other information is needed to help get the client to safety. In many cases, no further disclosure would be necessary.

Telehealth. Under California law, therapists who offer services via telemedicine are legally required to first obtain specific consent for telemedicine (the consent can be verbal or in writing) and document this in the client's file. Failure to do so is considered unprofessional conduct. While simply *scheduling* sessions by phone or email may not qualify as telehealth, providing therapy by phone would qualify, and providing therapy via videoconference certainly would. (Note that throughout this book, "telemedicine" and "telehealth" are used interchangeably.)

HIPAA requirements. Under the Health Insurance Portability and Accountability Act (HIPAA), CSWs covered by the act have specific additional responsibilities to protect the privacy of client records. Among the requirements:

- Designating a privacy official
- Informing clients and staff of privacy policy and procedures
- Disciplining staff members who violate privacy or security rules
- Repairing harmful effects of privacy violations
- Maintaining safeguards against the release of private information
- Having complaint procedures for violations of privacy
- Ensuring confidentiality of electronic health information
- Protecting against threats to information security
- Notifying the department of Health and Human Services of breaches of unsecured health information
- Getting client permission before communicating via unsecured email

Obviously, memorizing that whole list would take a fair amount of brain space. It may work best to simply recall that under HIPAA, CSWs need to have and enforce specific policies to protect the security and confidentiality of health information, and that clients are to be informed of the relevant policies. Most CSWs covered under HIPAA provide clients with a Notice of Privacy Policies that outlines how private information is gathered and used.

There is a specific category of documentation that HIPAA calls "psychotherapy notes," which are a therapist's notes documenting or analyzing conversation with a client that happens in a private psychotherapy session. Within this definition, psychotherapy notes cannot include information like session start and stop times, diagnosis, progress, treatment plans, symptoms, interventions, or prognosis. Psychotherapy notes, as defined under HIPAA, must be kept separate from the rest of the client file and are not considered part of the client record. However, under state law, these records would still be subject to subpoena.[6]

Preparing for the 2019 California Clinical Social Work Law & Ethics Exam

Sample Questions *See page 116 for answers and rationales*

1. A clinical social worker receives a request from a former client for their complete therapy records. The client's treatment occurred four years ago. When the CSW locates the former client's file, the CSW finds that the file is disorganized, and consists mostly of brief, handwritten notes. The CSW, whose current record-keeping is much improved, is embarrassed by the state of this old file. How should the CSW address their legal responsibilities in this case?

   a. Only agree to provide the client a written treatment summary in lieu of the full record.
   b. Recreate the handwritten notes in a more structured, typed format, adding details as needed. Discard the handwritten notes and provide the updated record within 10 days of the client's request.
   c. Refuse to release the file, on the grounds that it may be damaging to the CSW's relationship with the former client.
   d. Release the file in its current form, and offer to address any questions the former client may have.

2. A client asks whether her 75-year-old mother can be part of her therapy. The mother speaks English, but can only read and write in her native language, which you as the therapist are not familiar with. You believe that including the mother in the therapy may be helpful to the client. You should:

   a. Have the mother sign your informed consent form and join the therapy.
   b. Verbally discuss the process, risks, and benefits of therapy with the mother to help her decide whether to join the therapy, and document the discussion and her response.
   c. Refer the mother to a therapist who speaks her native language, and ask the client to sign a Release of Information form authorizing you to speak to that therapist.
   d. Ask the mother to teach you her native language so that you can provide all appropriate paperwork in her language.

Confidentiality & privilege

Privacy is a cornerstone of the therapeutic relationship. Unless a client can trust their therapist to keep information from therapy private, the client is unlikely to openly share their emotional struggles. CSWs are both legally and ethically required to maintain client confidentiality – that is, to keep all information from therapy private, including even the existence of a therapeutic relationship – unless a specific exception to confidentiality applies. Privacy is so important that even courts cannot usually access information from therapy: Communications between therapist and client are typically considered privileged communications, meaning they cannot be used in court. Again, though, there are several exceptions to this general standard.

Understanding confidentiality K1-2

Laws about confidentiality. Unless a specific exception to confidentiality applies, CSWs are legally required to keep the content of therapy confidential. This means that they do not share any information about clients, including even the existence of a therapeutic relationship, with outsiders.

Laws about disclosure. While confidentiality is the default state, a number of legal exceptions to confidentiality exist. In fact, there are more than 20 instances in state law where confidentiality can or must be broken, and information shared with outside persons or agencies.

Those instances where confidentiality *can* be broken are less relevant, as therapists will typically err on the side of confidentiality unless otherwise required by law. However, there may be instances where a therapist breaks confidentiality because the legally *can* do so and they believe it is in the best interest of the client to do so.

More commonly, though, the times when a CSW breaks confidentiality are limited to those times when the law requires it. These times can be generally broken down into five categories:

- Suspected child abuse
- Suspected elder or dependent adult abuse
- Danger to self or others
- Legal authorization, such as a court order or client release
- Other, less common instances where disclosure is required

The first four categories will be discussed in greater detail below. As a CSW, you need to be keenly aware of them. The fifth category – those less common instances where disclosure is required – includes an investigation by a board, commission, or administrative agency; a lawful request from an arbitrator or arbitration panel; a coroner's investigation of client's death; and a national security investigation. These instances rarely come up in therapy (if I were you, I wouldn't try to memorize those instances). In the event of a national security investigation, CSWs not only are required to turn over client records, but are legally prohibited from informing the client that they have done so.

Exceptions to confidentiality: Child abuse K18-19

Laws about reporting child abuse. CSWs are **mandated reporters** of suspected child abuse when serving in our professional roles. In other words, we are required to report abuse we observe or suspect while in the office, but are not required to report abuse we observe or suspect at the grocery store, at home, or in other non-professional settings.

Your mandated reporting responsibilities are triggered when, in your professional role, you develop **reasonable suspicion** that a minor has been abused. Reasonable suspicion is a specific term with a specific meaning. As the law is written, if another CSW with similar training and experience, when presented with the same information, would reasonably suspect that abuse had taken place, then so should you. You do not need to be certain that the abuse happened in order to reasonably suspect it – for example, you do not need to have personally observed injuries to suspect physical abuse.

There are five types of abuse that must be reported, and one that operates on a permissive reporting standard. The kinds of abuse that *must* be reported are:

- **Physical abuse.** Anyone who willfully causes an injury to a child or engages in cruel or unusual corporal punishment is committing physical abuse. There is some common mythology about what does and does not qualify as physical abuse, so it's best to consider the specific legal standard: *willfully causing an injury.* Accidents are generally not abuse, unless the accident resulted from endangerment, which is covered below. Striking a child with an open hand *can* be physical abuse if it leaves an injury such as a bruise. Striking a child with an object is not considered abuse if it does not leave an injury.
- **Sexual abuse.** This category includes sexual assault, sexual exploitation, and what the law calls "lewd and lascivious acts." When minors engage in consensual heterosexual intercourse, the therapist must consider their ages: If one partner is 14 years old or older, and the other is under 14, the therapist must report. Also, if one partner is under 16 and the other is 21 or older, the therapist must report. Otherwise, the therapist should consider the age and maturational levels of the partners in assessing their capacity to consent and the nature of the relationship (i.e., is it exploitive or otherwise abusive) when deciding whether to report. When minors consensually engage in oral sex, anal sex, or object penetration, the current reporting standard is unclear.[7] As such, this is unlikely to appear on your licensing exam. Of course, non-consensual oral sex, anal, object penetration, or intercourse will always be reportable when a minor is involved. "Lewd and lascivious acts" refers to other, non-penetrative sexual acts, such as manual stimulation of a partner. For these acts, if a minor under 14 is involved, they are always reportable. If a minor who is 14 or 15 is involved *and their partner is 10 or more years older,* the acts are reportable. Lewd and lascivious acts are not reportable as child abuse if the child is 16 or older.

- **Willful harm or endangerment.** Any person causing a child "unjusitifiable physical pain or mental suffering," or any caregiver who allows it to happen, is committing child abuse.
- **Neglect.** Even if it happens by accident, children are being neglected if their basic needs for adequate food, clothing, shelter, medical care, or supervision are not being met. A child *does not need to have suffered actual harm* for a report of neglect to be made. Note that a parent's informed medical choices, including choices to refuse medical treatment based on religious belief, are not neglect. However, the specific language of the law surrounding religious-based refusals of medical treatment requires that the child at least have been *examined* by a physician.
- **Abuse in out-of-home care.** This is given its own category for reporting purposes. It applies to kids who are physically injured or killed in child-care or school settings.

In addition to those types of abuse, **emotional abuse** operates on a *permissive* reporting standard, which means that you can report this if you choose to, but you are not required to. Children who witness domestic violence are sometimes reported as victims of emotional abuse.

Once you have developed reasonable suspicion, there are specific **timeframes for abuse reporting** that must be followed. You must make a report by phone to your local child protective agency immediately and follow up with a written report within 36 hours. This timeframe does not change for nights, weekends, or holidays.

Indicators of child abuse. Since the reasonable suspicion standard relies on CSWs having a shared understanding of when abuse should be reported, it is critical that CSWs are aware of common physical and behavioral indicators of abuse and neglect. While none of these indicators *by themselves* would lead to a conclusion of abuse or neglect, they should lead a CSW to *consider* whether abuse or neglect may be taking place. Common physical indicators include:

- Unexplained bruises
- Unexplained burns
- Unexplained fractures or cuts

What You Need to Know

- Evidence of delayed or inappropriate treatment for injuries
- Multiple injuries in various stages of healing
- Injury or trauma to genital area
- Sexually transmitted disease
- Pain, swelling, itching, bruising, or bleeding in genital area
- Unattended medical needs
- Consistent hunger or poor hygiene
- Consistent lack of supervision[8]

Notably, the law specifically states that the pregnancy of a minor, in and of itself, is *not* sufficient grounds to report suspected abuse. This remains true regardless of the age of the minor.

Common behavioral indicators of abuse and neglect include the following. As with all child and adolescent behaviors, a therapist must be especially cautious not to reach premature conclusions on the basis of behavioral indicators alone, as there are a number of potential causes for each of these that would *not* indicate abuse. However, these behaviors should get a therapist's attention:

- Sudden withdrawn behavior
- Self-destructive behavior
- Bizarre explanations for injuries
- Shying away from contact with familiar adults
- Sleep disturbances, including nightmares or flashbacks
- Substance use
- Anger and rage
- Aggressive, disruptive, or illegal behavior
- Frequent absence or tardiness from school or other activities
- Consistent fatigue or listlessness
- Stealing food
- Extreme need for affection
- Extreme loneliness[9]

Exceptions to confidentiality: Elder and dependent adult abuse K14-17

Laws about reporting elder and dependent adult abuse. Under California law, you must report any time you observe, suspect, or have knowledge of elder or dependent adult abuse. An elder is anyone age 65 or older who resides in California. A dependent adult is anyone age 18 to 64 who resides in California and has physical or mental limitations that restrict their ability to carry out normal activities or protect their own rights. Anyone admitted as an inpatient in a hospital or other 24-hour health care facility is, by definition, a dependent adult.

Reportable types of abuse include:

- **Physical abuse, which includes willful over- or under-medication.** Be careful with this, though — an elder reporting that they are in pain does not mean they are being abused. As long as they are being given the correct amount of medication prescribed by their doctor, it would simply call for a referral back to the client's physician to make any necessary adjustments in medication dosage or type. Various forms of sexual abuse are also included here as physical abuse.
- **Financial abuse.** This category is not a form of child abuse, but does apply to elders and dependent adults.
- **Abduction.** Specifically, the law refers to an elder or dependent adult being taken *outside of California*, or prevented from returning, against their will.
- **Isolation.** Elders who are physically restrained from seeing visitors, or who are being prevented from receiving mail, phone calls, or visitors (when the elder wants to see the visitor), are being isolated. In rare instances, a health condition may make limitations on mail and phone calls clinically appropriate, but there should be good medical documentation for such a decision, and other normal contact should not be restricted.
- **Abandonment.** Caretakers accept responsibility for the adults in their care. Abandonment occurs when a caretaker deserts their

patient or gives up on their caretaking responsibilities when a reasonable person would not have done so.
- **Neglect, including self-neglect.** This is reportable not so that the elder or dependent adult will be punished, but so that they can be moved to a higher level of care if it is appropriate to do so.

Unlike child abuse laws, elder and dependent adult abuse reporting laws include permissive reporting of any other form of abuse not otherwise defined in the law. This gives a CSW broad latitude to report behaviors that the CSW considers to be abusive or exploitative, even if those behaviors do not fit neatly into any of the categories listed.

Similar to child abuse reporting, you do not need to have heard a direct report of abuse from the victim in order to develop suspicion that abuse has taken place. However, unlike child abuse reporting laws, the laws on reporting elder and dependent adult abuse say that **if you do hear of abuse directly from the victim, you *must* report it.** There is only a very narrow exception, for when the person has been diagnosed with dementia or another form of mental illness that would impact their memory, there is no other evidence of the abuse, *and* the therapist does not believe the abuse occurred.

The **timeframes for reporting** elder or dependent adult abuse changed considerably in 2013, becoming much more complex. If the abuse did *not* take place in a long-term care facility, then a phone report of the abuse must be made immediately to Adult Protective Services or another local agency authorized to receive adult abuse reports. You then must follow up with a written report within two working days. (If the abuse happened within a long-term care facility, the rules are much more complicated, sometimes requiring duplicate or triplicate reporting, and with varied reporting timeframes.) Recent state law allows for elder and dependent adult abuse reports to be made via Internet, in which case the Internet report should be done immediately, and it replaces both the phone *and* written reports.

Indicators of elder and dependent adult abuse. Common indicators of elder abuse include the following. As is the case with child abuse, it may be inappropriate to conclude that abuse has occurred based solely on an indicator here, as each of these can be caused by incidents that would *not* qualify as abuse. However, they can raise a therapist's suspicion, and suspicion is the standard for reporting:

- Physical or sexual abuse
    - Unexplained bruises, welts, or scars
    - Broken bones, sprains, dislocations
    - Restraint injuries (marks on wrists)
    - Unexplained bleeding or injury to genitals
    - Sexually transmitted disease
    - Medication over- or under-dosing relative to prescription
- Abandonment or neglect
    - Unusual weight loss
    - Poor nutrition or dehydration
    - Poor hygiene
    - Unsanitary or unsafe living environment
    - Inappropriate clothing (inadequate for cold weather)
    - Lack of needed medical aids, such as glasses
- Financial abuse
    - Sudden changes in financial status
    - Valuable items or cash missing from residence
    - Unpaid bills when the person has money to pay them
    - Unusual financial activity, or activity the person could not have done (e.g., large withdrawals, ATM withdrawal by hospital inpatient)
    - Sudden appearance of unnecessary goods or services
    - Signatures on checks do not match the person's
- Unusual caregiver behavior (suggests risk of abuse of any type)
    - Threatening, belittling, or controlling behavior
    - Deserting
    - Burnout (can be evidenced by depression, substance use, poor resilience, or perception that caregiving is burdensome)[10]

It is important for CSWs to be aware that stress and burnout are common among caregivers. These indicate a risk of abuse, but may also simply mean that the caregiver needs some time away from their responsibilities. Caregiving is difficult, particularly if the person being cared for has severe illness or dementia, is socially isolated, is physically aggressive, or has a history of domestic violence. These factors place the person at greater risk of abuse.

Exceptions to confidentiality: Danger to self or others K20-25, 76

Identifying need for hospitalization. Under state law, an individual can be hospitalized against their will if they are a danger to others, are a danger to themselves, or are gravely disabled. In such instances, the person is taken to a hospital (or other county-designated facility) for assessment for up to 72 hours, which you may know as a "72-hour hold" or a "5150."[11]

Legal requirements for initiating involuntary hospitalization. When a CSW believes hospitalization is necessary, having a client go voluntarily is usually preferable to the process of involuntary hospitalization. However, if the CSW believes the client has a mental disorder that is causing them to be a danger to themselves or others or is gravely disabled, and the client refuses voluntary treatment, the CSW can begin the process of involuntary hospitalization. In order for a client to be hospitalized against their will, a therapist must be able to cite specific facts (client words, appearance or behaviors) supporting the dangerousness of the client, and the conclusions the therapist drew from those facts.

Ultimately, it is up to a professional at the facility designated by the county to receive involuntary holds to determine whether the client is to be involuntarily hospitalized. If that professional agrees, the client can be initially held for up to 72 hours.[12]

Laws about confidentiality in situations of client danger to self or others. Danger to self or others is commonly understood as an exception to confidentiality under the law. The *Tarasoff v. California Board of Regents* case established that danger to a reasonably identifiable victim outweighs client confidentiality. A CSW dealing with a client who poses an imminent danger of serious bodily harm to reasonably identifiable victims must take reasonable steps to resolve the threat, which necessarily include breaking confidentiality. (See "Duty to protect law" below.) When a client is suicidal, the *Bellah v. Greenson* case established that therapists have a responsibility to act to protect the client's safety, and this can involve breaking confidentiality to have the client hospitalized if needed. If a client poses a general danger to others because of a mental health condition, *Tarasoff* does not apply but the therapist still can move to have the client involuntarily hospitalized if needed.

In each of these instances, the CSW breaks confidentiality. The CSW shares information about therapy with others who are involved in resolving the immediate danger. Even in these situations, though, the CSW should share only the information necessary to resolve the immediate threat.

If a *Tarasoff* situation arises where the therapist is able to resolve the immediate danger *without* notifying law enforcement, the CSW still must inform law enforcement of the threat within 24 hours. This relatively recent law was enacted to help law enforcement put potentially dangerous individuals into a database that would prevent them from buying guns.

Methods and criteria to identify when a client poses danger to self or others. Thankfully, there are good, brief ways of assessing clients who may pose a danger to themselves or someone else. Assessments for suicide and violence to others tend to focus on the following factors:

- **Ideation (thoughts).** Is the person actively thinking about harming themselves or someone else? For suicidality, are they romanticizing what their death would be like, for them or for others around them?
- **Planning.** Do they have a specific plan for how they would hurt themselves or someone else? Is it immediate?
- **Intent.** Does the person intend to commit violence? How sure are they? Some clients will fantasize about violence or death without any intent to ever act on these fantasies.
- **Access to means.** How easy would it be to carry out the plan? If they are considering suicide or homicide by gun, is there a gun in the house?
- **Past experience.** Have they attempted suicide or been violent with others before? How? Note that *previous suicide attempts* is the strongest risk factor for future attempts.
- **Protective factors.** What are the reasons the person has not hurt themselves or someone else so far? What would prevent them from suicide or violence in the future?

Demographic factors are also important to keep in mind, though these are not predictive of violence. While suicide is a leading cause of death among adolescents (because other causes of death are not common at this age), statistically, the highest risk for suicide is among the elderly (85+) and the middle-aged (45-64). Men are at higher risk than women. Whites and Native Americans have the highest suicide rates among ethnic groups.

Duty to protect law. You are probably familiar with *Tarasoff v. California Board of Regents*, the court case that established a therapist's responsibility to act when a client poses an imminent danger of serious bodily harm to a reasonably identifiable victim or victims. In such instances, CSWs have a legal obligation known as "duty to protect." While this is not technically a duty to *warn* (and in rare instances, it might be inappropriate to warn the intended victim, such as times when doing so might trigger the victim to commit a violent act), the most common methods of protecting potential victims are to notify the victims and law enforcement of the threat. You also have additional protection from liability when you make reasonable efforts to notify both the victim and law enforcement.

The law does *not* require you to report or otherwise act on threats to property. However, threats to property are not considered privileged communication under the law (more on Privilege is below), which CAMFT has interpreted to mean that therapists may share such a threat with law enforcement, the property owners, or others as needed to prevent the danger.

Indicators of intent to harm. Obviously, the strongest indicator of a client's intent to harm someone is when they tell you directly that they intend to harm someone. However, this is not the only indicator a therapist should be aware of. Third-party reports of a client intending to harm another person may be treated similarly to direct reports, if the therapist believes that the third party is a trustworthy reporter. Threats made in writing or by other means may be considered evidence of intent to harm. Indirect statements such as "after today, she won't be around anymore" may also be reasonable indicators, based on the CSW's knowledge of the client. Threatening behaviors may also qualify. Clients who are actively using drugs or alcohol may present heightened danger to potential victims.

Exceptions to confidentiality: Legal authorization

Another category of exceptions to confidentiality is triggered when there is an appropriate legal authorization to release information that would otherwise remain confidential. Clients may request that their records be released to a third party, using what is commonly called a Release of Information form. Judges might order the release of records. More information on these instances can be found in the section on "Understanding Privilege" a couple of pages ahead.

Managing confidentiality K70, 74-75

Ethical standards. NASW requires CSWs to specifically inform clients of the limits of confidentiality as soon as possible in the social worker-client relationship. Clients also may benefit from reminders of these limits during the course of services.

In addition, throughout the course of treatment there are multiple standards that relate to CSWs' responsibility to keep client information private. Consultations, recordkeeping, telemedicine, supervision, teaching/presentation, and preparation for moving or closing a practice are *all* to be done in ways that protect client confidentiality, unless a specific exception applies or the client has granted permission for their information to be shared.

Managing the impact of confidentiality issues. When it is possible and appropriate to do so, CSWs are expected to discuss disclosures of confidential information with clients *before* the disclosure is made. This discussion should include considerations of the potential consequences of that disclosure.

Particularly if a CSW has been legally obligated to share information from treatment, a discussion with the client about what information was shared, with whom, and why can help minimize negative impacts on the therapeutic relationship. Such a discussion can also serve to remind the client of the limits of confidentiality, and of the therapist's commitment to protecting the safety of any others involved. For example, if a report of suspected child abuse has been made, the CSW may want to discuss the role that a CSW plays in larger society in protecting vulnerable populations from suspected abuse. Ultimately, a conversation like this can refocus client and therapist on the therapeutic process and (hopefully) repair any harm done to the therapeutic relationship.

Confidentiality can be impacted by the client unit, treatment type, and involvement of outside systems. When a CSW is providing treatment to a couple or family, the CSW needs to inform clients of (and abide by) the CSW's or employer's policy for handling individual secrets. The CSW cannot guarantee that family members will respect one another's privacy. The same applies in group therapy, where the CSW is expected to initiate discussions of group members' responsibilities to one another, including respect for each other's privacy. Again, CSWs cannot guarantee that group members will abide by the group's policy. When outside systems are involved in treatment, they may request (or require) that the CSW provide regular updates on the therapy process. CSWs talk with clients about such disclosures before they occur whenever possible, including discussion of their impacts on the client and the therapy process.

Understanding privilege K3-6

Privilege refers to information that can be excluded from court proceedings. Normally, all communications between a therapist and their client are considered privileged communications, meaning that they cannot be used in court. Other examples of communication that is usually privileged include communication between spouses, and communication between an attorney and their client. Privilege is specifically a *legal* issue, outlined in California law.

This is particularly important in therapy. Clients need to be able to trust that information they have shared with their therapist about mental health symptoms or other emotional problems will not be used against them in court; if that risk exists, clients will understandably be less open with their therapists about struggles in the clients' lives.

Clients generally hold their own privilege. In other words, only the client can waive their own right to privileged communication in most instances. Even when the client is a minor, the client is usually considered the holder of their own privilege, although the minor may not be allowed to *waive* privilege on their own. A judge may block a minor (or an adult, for that matter) from waiving privilege if the judge believes that waiving privilege is not in the person's best interest. In any case, it is never up to the therapist to determine whether privilege should be waived. That is up to the client, the client's guardian, another court appointee, or a judge.

Release of privileged information. By definition, privileged information cannot be used in a court proceeding. Privileged information may only be released in court if the client has waived privilege, or if a judge has determined that privilege does not apply, based on one or more of the exceptions spelled out in state law (see "Exceptions to privilege" starting on the next page).

Responding to a subpoena or court order. If a CSW receives a subpoena (a legal document requesting that the therapist produce records, appear in court, or both), there are specific steps the CSW is commonly advised to take. These include:

1. **Contact an attorney as soon as possible.** The CSW will benefit from legal guidance throughout this process.
2. **Assess the subpoena for its source and validity.** A subpoena *from a judge* is a court order – the CSW must obey it. A subpoena from a *private attorney* is different, and may be fought if the client chooses. Occasionally, your attorney may advise you to object to the subpoena, if there is something wrong with the subpoena itself or how it was delivered.
3. **Contact the client to determine their wishes.** Often, the client will freely authorize the CSW to release the records or appear in court. Sometimes, the client will prefer that the CSW assert privilege on the client's behalf, arguing that the therapist's records or testimony should not be made part of the court proceeding.
4. Unless the client has specifically waived privilege or a judge has determined that privilege does not apply, **assert privilege.** This is considered the appropriate default position for a CSW to take in the absence of other guidance from the client or the court.[13]

Of course, if the client does waive privilege, or if a court determines that privilege does not apply, you must comply with the subpoena.

Exceptions to privilege K26-31

Privilege refers to information that can be excluded from court proceedings. Normally, all communications between a therapist and their client are considered *privileged communications*, meaning that they cannot be used in court. However, there are a number of exceptions to this rule, including six that you may be specifically asked about on your exam:

1) The client makes their mental or emotional condition an issue in a lawsuit.
2) The client alleges breach of duty by the therapist.
3) Evaluation or therapy is taking place by court order.
4) A defendant in a criminal case requested the evaluation or therapy to determine their sanity.
5) The client is under age 16 and is the victim of a crime, and the therapist believes that disclosing that information is in the child's best interests.
6) The therapist was sought out for the purpose of committing a crime or avoiding detection after the fact.

Since each one of these exceptions gets its own Knowledge Statement in the Exam Plan, there is a strong likelihood you will be specifically asked to apply your knowledge of one or more of these.

What You Need to Know

Sample Questions *See page 118 for answers and rationales*

1. An elder client tells a CSW working in hospice care that the client was recently taken to a local religious gathering against her will by her 50-year-old daughter. The daughter is a member of the religious group. By the client's report, the daughter told her mother that "this might be good for you, being around people with good values" and did not bring the mother home when the mother said she was uncomfortable there. Furthermore, the daughter donated the cash in the client's purse to the religious group, despite the client's repeated statements to her daughter that the client did not support the group. How should the CSW respond to their legal obligations in this case?

   a. Report suspected elder abuse (specifically, kidnapping)
   b. Report suspected elder abuse (specifically, financial abuse)
   c. Report suspected elder abuse (specifically, emotional abuse)
   d. Report suspected elder abuse (specifically, isolation)

2. A 15-year-old girl is seeing a CSW individually for issues related to body image and self-esteem. Her parents provided consent for the therapy and pay for her sessions, but do not participate. The girl tells the CSW that she has been exploring her sexuality. While her parents were out of town, she had sexual intercourse with a friend's 19-year-old brother. A few days later, she had intercourse with another boy, an 18-year-old senior at her high school. The CSW should manage their legal responsibilities by:

   a. Reporting child abuse to the local child protective service agency
   b. Investigating to ensure that the sexual activity was not coerced or while under the influence of drugs or alcohol
   c. Notifying the parents of their daughter's high-risk sexual behavior
   d. Maintaining confidentiality

3. The client of a CSW is on trial for fraud. The client is accused of submitting false claims to the client's insurance company, including claims for sessions that did not actually take place. At the client's request, the CSW had provided superbills and related documentation to the client to support her insurance claims, including those for sessions that did not happen. The CSW is called upon to testify under court order. How can the CSW best address their legal responsibilities in this case?

    a. Refuse to share any information on the basis of therapist-client privilege
    b. Contact the client and determine how they wish to proceed
    c. Acknowledge that the overbilling occurred, but describe it as an administrative error rather than incriminating the client
    d. Provide specific and detailed testimony about the scheme

Treatment

Consideration of legal and ethical responsibilities does not stop at informed consent. Additional legal and ethical responsibilities can arise throughout therapy. While the Law and Ethics Exam is not focused on clinical skills, you may be asked questions that relate to your ability to address treatment issues in a manner that is consistent with legal and ethical responsibilities.

Technology K12 "delivery" portion, 111-113

Telemedicine laws. California and federal laws govern the delivery of services by telehealth. Under state law, clients must be informed about the use of telehealth and give their consent before telehealth services can be provided. The CSW must document that this consent was received.

When delivering services by telehealth, all of the laws regarding scope of practice, client confidentiality, and client rights to information and records continue to apply. CSWs must be particularly cautious when considering using telemedicine to treat clients located outside of California, as a California CSW license only governs services provided to clients located within the state at the time of service.

Under regulations adopted in 2016, California CSWs wishing to conduct therapy via telehealth need to take several specific steps. *At the start* of engaging a client in telehealth, the CSW must:

- Get specific telehealth consent (as noted above)
- Inform clients of the risks and limitations of telehealth services
- Provide the client with the CSW's licensure/registration information
- Document efforts to locate crisis resources local to the client

If that last one sounds a little stilted, that's because it is. A low-risk client wouldn't require the same effort to locate crisis resources local to them as a high-risk client would. So based on your assessment of client risk, you may locate crisis resources local to them just in case they're needed. Whatever you do in this area, it should be documented.

In addition to the steps above, the CSW must do the following *at each instance* of telehealth:

- Obtain and document the client's full name and current location (this should be an address, to confirm that you are qualified to provide services where they are)
- Assess whether the client is appropriate for telehealth (this may be based on their symptoms, and also may be based on the technology and privacy available to the client at that time)
- Use best practices for security and confidentiality

Ethical standards. The most recent revisions to the NASW Code of Ethics took effect January 1, 2018. Most of the revisions focused on technology-assisted services. Technology-specific obligations operate *on top of* all of the regular ethical requirements for social work, not in place of them. CSWs providing services via telemedicine are ethically obligated to:

- Inform clients of the risks and benefits specific to telemedicine
- Discuss policies regarding the use of technology
- Comply with all applicable legal standards for practice in the location where the social worker is *and* the location where the client is
- Avoid using technology for personal or non-work related communications with clients
- Protect confidentiality of technological communication and electronic records
- Notify clients of any breaches of confidential data

Limitations of telemedicine. The use of technology to connect with clients over great distances comes with some natural risks and limitations. Some clients (and some therapists) lack the technical skills needed to use technology in the delivery of mental health services. The technology may not be sufficient for the CSW to pick up on subtle cues that would otherwise be important to assess. The client may need services beyond what the therapist can provide through telemedicine. And of course, there is always the possibility that the technology will simply fail, leaving client and therapist disconnected. While technology may be a suitable method for working with many clients, CSWs must carefully assess whether telemedicine services are appropriate to the client's needs and abilities.

Potential for harm. In some cases, the use of technology in therapy has the potential to damage the client or the therapeutic relationship. Direct harm may come to the client if the CSW is unable to accurately assess the nature or severity of client symptoms, or changes to those symptoms, when seeing a client by phone or online. The client also may be harmed if the therapist is unable to provide needed local resources in an emergency, or if a session taking place by phone or Internet leads to breaches of confidentiality.

Even when the client is not directly harmed, the relationship between therapist and client can be damaged when technology is not used responsibly. Clients may perceive that the therapist is not as attendant to their needs, or unable to intervene with them in the ways they would in person. Unless a client is well-motivated for technology-based services, the CSW should carefully consider whether seeing the client in person would be a better fit.

Managing crises K77-78

Ethical obligations for protecting safety. The first standard in the NASW Code of Ethics defines social workers' primary responsibility as promoting the well-being of clients. Many other ethical standards logically stem from this responsibility. For example, CSWs normally recognize and respect a client's right to self-determination. However, the CSW may limit clients' right to self-determination if the CSW believes that the client poses (or would pose) a risk to themselves or others. As another example, confidentiality is not to be protected when disclosure would prevent a serious and foreseeable harm.

In addition to this responsibility to individual clients, social workers also have a responsibility to the larger community and society. CSWs are expected to provide appropriate professional services in public emergencies, and to actively work for the general well-being of society.

Procedures for managing safety needs. As a general rule, safety needs should be addressed through the *least intrusive means* necessary to resolve the concern. You wouldn't hospitalize a mildly depressed patient, after all. Here are a few procedures for managing safety needs, ranging from the least to the most intrusive. This is not a complete list, and the options here are not mutually exclusive; it may be appropriate to develop a safety plan *and* increase the frequency of contact with a client, for example.

- **Continue to assess.** In the absence of any specific safety concerns, the therapist would simply continue assessing for safety in future interactions with the client.
- **Consultation with the treatment team.** If you are participating on an interdisciplinary treatment team and have appropriate authorization to share information, it may be helpful to consult the team for their assessment of risk and to collaborate on methods for continued assessment and intervention.
- **More detailed assessment.** If a client suggests that their depression is deepening or that their hostility to others is increasing, but does not discuss any specific danger or threat, the therapist should assess the area of concern in more detail.
- **Development of a safety plan.** If a client has a history of safety issues, or is currently showing non-specific safety concerns (for example, a client with mild passive suicidality, but no plan or intent to harm themselves), a therapist may develop a safety plan. This plan lays out specific steps the client can take if their symptoms worsen. Steps usually follow a progression if early steps are unavailable or do not solve the problem. Steps may include contacting loved ones, contacting the therapist, contacting another on-duty therapist, and if these steps are unsuccessful, contacting a 24-hour crisis hotline or calling 911.
- **Increasing frequency of contact.** If you have been seeing a client weekly and you begin to have concerns about their safety, but those concerns do not rise to the level where more immediate intervention is needed, you may ask to see them more often, or for the client to check in by phone more regularly. You may also choose to increase the frequency of collateral contacts (with probation officers, family members, or others in the client's life).

- **Refer to a higher level of care.** Clients whose symptoms get worse or who become dangerous during outpatient psychotherapy may be better served through inpatient treatment.
- **Voluntary hospitalization.** Clients who pose an imminent danger to themselves or others and are willing to be assessed and treated voluntarily at a hospital will not be held there against their will. When a therapist is firm with a client that hospitalization is necessary, most clients will choose voluntary hospitalization over involuntary hospitalization.
- **Involuntary hospitalization.** If a client presents a major safety risk and is not willing to be hospitalized, a CSW may initiate the process of involuntary hospitalization. While most CSWs cannot invoke involuntary hospitalization, they can demand that a client be evaluated for a possible 72-hour hold.

Of course, if the safety concern is that the client poses an immediate danger of severe bodily harm to a reasonably identifiable victim, the appropriate procedure would be to notify the victim and law enforcement.

Scope of competence K41-45

Understanding scope of competence. Your scope of competence is defined by your education, training, and professional experience. Your scope of competence is unique to you and can change over time. Scope of competence is primarily an *ethical* issue, though practicing outside of one's scope of competence is considered unprofessional conduct in state law.

Knowing your own limitations. Just as it is important to be able to identify actions that would be out of the CSW scope of practice, it is also critical to understand when issues come before you that are outside your scope of competence. You can't possibly have training and experience for every possible situation you will encounter in your practice, so acknowledging limitations in your scope of competence is not a weakness. It is good professional behavior.

Need for consultation. When a situation comes up in therapy that is outside of a CSW's scope of competence, a responsible CSW will consult with a supervisor, treatment team, or others to determine what appropriate next steps would be. (As noted earlier, CSWs are expected to remain up to date on colleagues' expertise, such that the CSW can consult with an appropriate person.) In many cases, the therapist will work to expand their competence while continuing to work with the client. In other cases, a referral may be deemed more appropriate.

Protecting client rights in consultations. While consultations are a regular part of many CSWs' practices, it is important to be cautious in protecting client rights during such consultations. CSWs only share identifiable and confidential information about a client during a consultation if the client has given specific written consent. Even then, the CSW should only provide the information necessary for the consultation.

Expanding competence. If one's scope of competence is determined by education, training, and experience, then it makes sense that CSWs can expand into new areas of practice, or improve their competence in existing ones, by getting additional education, training, and experience.

Responsibility to remain current. The CSW field is constantly growing and changing, with new treatment models and new scientific developments occurring on a regular basis. The training and experience that make you competent to work with a certain problem today may be considered outdated and inaccurate 10 years from now. CSWs have an ethical responsibility to remain current with new developments in the profession, through the use of education, training, and supervised experience. This is part of the reason why licensed CSWs are required to get continuing education hours in each license renewal cycle.

Working with multiple clients K69, 73

Identifying the "client." CSWs are ethically obligated to clarify at the beginning of therapy which person or persons are considered clients, and the nature of the relationship the therapist will have with each person involved in treatment. There is a meaningful difference between a partner or family member *visiting* treatment, where they might offer input or moral support to a client's problem, and being a *client*, where they may be directly involved in therapeutic interventions. Whether someone is a client or not will impact the social worker's responsibilities to that person. If work with a family creates the potential for a conflict of interests, the CSW should take steps to minimize that conflict.

Confidentiality. When working with couples or families, confidentiality becomes a key concern. If a client calls between sessions and informs the therapist of a secret, does the therapist have the right to bring that information up in a couple or family session?

The NASW Code of Ethics requires that CSWs inform clients of applicable policies regarding the handling of individual confidences. Some CSWs and agencies support a no-secrets policy, where individual confidences will *not* be upheld. Others prefer a limited-secrets policy, believing this is better for accurate assessment of the couple or family. In either case, the CSW should ensure that all individuals in the couple or family being treated are aware of the policy, and the CSW should then stick to that policy.

In couple, family, or group therapy, CSWs should seek agreement among participants as to their responsibilities to each other. Such clients should be warned that others participating in treatment with them may not honor those agreements. Some CSWs ask group members to sign an agreement that they will respect the privacy of the group.

Preserving the therapeutic relationship. Of course, it would not be possible to list all of the factors that can influence the therapeutic relationship in couple, family, or group therapy. Nor is that necessary for an exam about legal and ethical practice. Lots of things can influence the relationship, not all of which are foreseeable. If the CSW keeps client welfare and the preservation of the therapeutic relationship paramount, the CSW will be able to manage most of these factors easily.

Consider two examples: In the first example, a CSW doing couple therapy begins to feel hostility from one of the partners, and is not sure why. The CSW asks the other partner whether it would be ok to meet alone with the hostile partner for a few minutes, and the other partner agrees. During this time, the hostile partner reveals that she is concerned the therapist is siding with her spouse over her. While this was not the CSW's intent, the CSW is able to change behavior moving forward, and offers and apology to the hostile partner.

In the second example, a CSW doing family therapy with a mother, father, and their two adolescent girls assesses that the girls' acting out behavior appears to be related to conflict in the parental subsystem. The CSW discusses with the family the possibility of changing the treatment modality to focus on couple work. While the CSW reminds the family that he enjoys having them all come in, he believes the girls have done their job, and now it is time for him to do his in treating the family's core issue.

In each of these cases, the therapist took steps to support client welfare and the therapeutic relationship, when it would have easily been possible for therapy to go down an unproductive path. A CSW should be able to address therapeutic issues related to their role, the modality of treatment, and the involvement of outsiders openly with clients.

Treatment involving multiple systems or third parties. The NASW Code of Ethics encourages CSWs to revisit discussions of confidentiality with clients when appropriate. This is especially important when treatment involves multiple systems or third parties. In some cases, providing services to an adolescent may mean involving their teacher, their religious leader, their family therapist, and others. Everyone involved should be clear about what the CSW's role is and what the third parties' roles are in the treatment, and how information may be shared among treatment providers and others. Managing privacy and confidentiality in these situations can be a complex task. Of course, clients should give permission before third parties are brought in to treatment, and should be made aware that they can revoke this permission at any time.

Termination and referrals K49, 95-101

Ethical considerations with interrupting or terminating. There are times when interrupting or terminating therapy is appropriate or necessary, even when the goals of therapy have not been reached. You may become seriously ill, or need to step away from your practice to care for loved ones. The client may suddenly be called to a military deployment or a new job out of state. Your clinic may lose its funding. While we all hope these situations will not occur, the reality is that they often do, and a CSW is ethically required to be ready for such abrupt shifts. A CSW also must take appropriate steps when this kind of situation does happen.

CSWs are ethically required to take reasonable steps to ensure continuity of services in the event that they become suddenly incapacitated or otherwise unavailable. These procedures may include emergency contact numbers where clients may reach the therapist or others able to take over client care. CSWs commonly have what is called a *professional will*, which lays out issues like who will take over client care in the event of the therapist's serious injury or death. The person assigned to take over client care must be given access to records so that they can contact clients to let them know of the change; for this reason, many CSWs include an authorization in their informed consent agreement letting clients know that a professional will exists and having clients agree that their records may be forwarded when necessary.

Having these plans in place minimizes the harm that may come to clients when a therapist is suddenly unavailable. However, treatment interruptions or sudden terminations are not always due to something happening to the therapist.

Whenever treatment must be interrupted or terminated, regardless of whether it is because of something happening to the client, the therapist, the clinic, or the larger social context, CSWs have ethical responsibilities to *non-abandonment* and appropriate *continuity of care*. Non-abandonment simply means that clients in need of continued services typically should not be left to fend for themselves; if treatment with the current CSW must be interrupted or ended, the CSW still has a responsibility to ensure that crisis needs are addressed and that any potential for harm due to the change in treatment is minimized. Continuity of care means that the client is able to receive continued care with another provider appropriate to their needs; most commonly, this means providing referrals that are local to the client, within their financial means, and able to treat the client's specific problem type and severity.

Social workers are ethically prohibited from terminating services in order to pursue a social, financial, or sexual relationship with a client.

Knowledge of referrals/resources to provide continuity of care. In order to make referrals when necessary, a CSW must be aware of local resources that can provide continuity of care to clients if therapy is suddenly stopped. Many CSWs maintain referral lists that include local hospitals and crisis resources, low-fee clinics, psychiatrists, other providers whose services are similar to those of the CSW, and additional community resources.

Indicators of need to terminate or refer. The clearest indication that it is time to terminate therapy is, of course, when it is clear that the client has reached their treatment goals, and no new goals have emerged. Even in the absence of having reached the goals of treatment, if a client regularly comes in appearing to no longer be in distress, this can indicate that the client is ready to be done with therapy. Ongoing, careful monitoring and discussion with clients about their changing needs can help determine whether and when termination or additional referrals may be necessary.

The CSW should also refer out, or terminate existing services, if:

- The CSW is not able to provide competent services due to impairment
- There is risk of a conflict of interests
- There is a dual relationship that is likely to create risk of exploitation or impair the CSW's clinical judgment

Of course, referrals are appropriate for addressing client needs that the CSW cannot immediately address. Client reports of medical symptoms suggest a need for a referral to a physician. Other needs that the CSW cannot meet, but that appear relevant to the client's functioning, may be best met through appropriate referrals.

Client is not benefiting. Even if the goals of therapy have not been reached, it is appropriate to terminate therapy if it is clear that the client is not benefiting from treatment. Further deterioration of functioning is a clear indication of treatment failure. A lack of improvement in symptoms may or may not indicate a lack of benefit from treatment; if a client entered therapy on a downward trend, simply stabilizing them and keeping them out of hospitalization can be considered a benefit. Ultimately, though, clients should experience a benefit from being in therapy. If, by their own report or by therapist or other observation of client behavior, they are not improving, termination should be considered – with referrals given if symptoms still warrant treatment.

Managing termination. It is generally understood that a good termination process starts at the *beginning* of services, with therapist and client reaching clear agreement on what the goals of the services are and what improvements will lead to a determination that services can end. Discussions of progress toward termination should be a regular part of therapy. Once it is clear that termination is appropriate, a responsible CSW will provide advance notice of termination, and in one or more termination sessions, the CSW will take steps to prevent a relapse of symptoms, recognize the gains the client has made in therapy, and provide appropriate referrals for any additional needed care.

Preventing abandonment or neglect. A termination process that is done too quickly or without appropriate referrals can be considered client abandonment. There may be times when a therapist needs to end therapy abruptly, either due to a medical illness, client job transfer or deployment, or for other reasons. In such circumstances, the CSW (or, in the case of the CSW's illness, someone designated by the CSW) should offer as much advance notice of termination as possible, make appropriate referrals, and follow up to ensure the clients are able to obtain continued services.

Therapeutic Relationship K71

Factors impacting the relationship. The relationship between therapist and client is generally considered the most powerful driver of change. This relationship can be impacted by a wide range of factors, some positive and some negative. Clients want a therapist they can like and trust, and trust is sometimes more difficult when outside systems are involved in therapy. The CSW can facilitate the therapeutic relationship by emphasizing client self-determination and setting clear boundaries and expectations.

Carl Rogers' principles of accurate empathy, unconditional positive regard, and self-congruence can help CSWs build strong relationships with clients. While some studies suggest that clients want a therapist who looks like them (in terms of matching race or gender), these effects generally wear off quickly as clients' initial impressions of a therapist are overtaken by their actual experience.

CSWs should be attuned and responsive to factors that may be negatively impacting the therapeutic relationship. If the CSW reaches a point where they no longer believe the relationship can work to facilitate effective treatment, the client should be referred to another service provider.

Preparing for the 2019 California Clinical Social Work Law & Ethics Exam

Sample Questions *See page 121 for answers and rationales*

1. A client has cancelled three of the last seven scheduled sessions with an LCSW, and been a no-show for the other four. Each time, the client has promised to pay any balance charged, and to come in for a session the following week. The LCSW finds herself irritated with the client's behavior, going so far as to warn the client two weeks ago that she would simply close the client's case and refer out if the client didn't come in. The client was a no-show for the next two scheduled sessions. Even before this long series of missed appointments, the LCSW found herself personally disliking the client. How should the LCSW manage her ethical responsibilities in this case?

    a. Meaningfully assess for crisis, and continue as the client's treatment provider if necessary.
    b. Close the case, providing the client with appropriate referrals to other providers.
    c. Provide the client at least two additional warnings, one of which must be in writing, prior to terminating therapy.
    d. Seek consultation to address countertransference, and continue to work toward the client more regularly attending therapy.

2. As a client leaves a CSW's office, the CSW believes the client poses a serious danger to the client's spouse. (The client had been making threats in session about what he would do to her.) The CSW, knowing the couple lives roughly 30 minutes from the CSW's office, calls the client immediately, and is able to resolve the danger. The client disavows any continued plan to harm his spouse, and apologizes to the CSW for "getting so out of hand." What does the CSW need to do to resolve the CSW's legal responsibility?

    a. Notify the spouse and law enforcement immediately
    b. Notify the spouse immediately
    c. Notify law enforcement within 24 hours
    d. Notify the local child protective services agency

3. A clinical social worker is working with a same-sex couple in therapy. One partner expresses that he is feeling hostile toward the CSW. The CSW asks to meet briefly with that partner alone. During the individual discussion, the partner says that he feels the CSW is siding against him, interrupting him, and generally not respecting his complaints about the relationship. The CSW is surprised by this, and begins to wonder what else the CSW has been missing in session. How should the CSW handle their responsibilities in this case?

    a. Recognize each individual as a unique client, and offer to see the partners individually if they prefer.
    b. Discontinue treatment, as the therapeutic relationship has been corrupted, and refer to at least three therapists competent in working with same-sex couples.
    c. Conceptualize the client's reaction as paranoia, as it is inconsistent with the therapist's experience. Integrate this into the CSW's understanding of the dynamics of the relationship.
    d. Work to restore the therapeutic relationship with the partner, and consider finding consultation or supervision for this case.

The business of social work

For better or worse, the practice of clinical social work is a business. The fact that clients (or others) are paying money for mental health services means that CSWs must be responsible in the fees they charge, the disclosures they make, and generally in how the business side of the practice is handled. This section focuses on legal and ethical standards relating to business issues, such as payment for services and advertising.

Setting and collecting fees K114, 116-118

Determining fees. There are many factors you can consider when setting fees, such as a client's income, the fees generally charged for services in your area, your own qualifications, and so on. There are three particular things you *can't* do when determining fees:

- You can't enter into an agreement with other independent practitioners or clinics to set a common fee (or common minimum fee) in your area. This would be a violation of antitrust law.
- You can't set different fees based on race, national origin, or any other protected class in anti-discrimination rules.
- You can't set fees that are exploitive (i.e., high fees that take advantage of clients' vulnerability or wealth).

Fees must be fair, reasonable, and aligned with the services that clients are paying for. You can raise or lower fees whenever you wish, even for existing clients. You simply need to make sure that your fee changes are within the rules listed above.

Bartering. Bartering – that is, exchanging clinical services for some other product or service, rather than money – comes with a lot of potential problems. There is risk of exploitation if the market value of the goods or services the client offers as payment exceeds the usual fee the CSW charges. There is also the risk that the therapy relationship will be impacted, if the therapist particularly likes or dislikes the goods or services received, or if they hold strong sentimental value for the client.

In spite of those problems, bartering is not completely prohibited. The NASW Code of Ethics allows CSWs to "explore and [...] participate in bartering only in very limited circumstances."[14] Under the NASW code, bartering is only acceptable if *all* of these conditions are met (reformatted here into a list):

"(a) such arrangements are an accepted practice among professionals in the local community,
(b) considered to be essential for the provision of services,
(c) negotiated without coercion, and
(d) entered into at the client's initiative and
(e) with the client's informed consent."[15]

As a general rule, you should not enter into a bartering arrangement with clients. If bartering ultimately presents a problem, the burden is on the CSW to show that the bartering arrangement was not detrimental to the client. However, under the limited circumstances described above, there may be rare instances when bartering for services is preferable to interrupting or discontinuing treatment.

Collecting unpaid balances. CSWs are within their legal rights to collect unpaid balances, and even to use collection agencies or courts when necessary to do so. Of course, this should be handled with care and sensitivity, and only after other avenues for collecting balances have failed. Naturally, the collection agency or court should not be given any clinical information about the client.

Continuation of treatment. The NASW Code of Ethics goes so far as to specifically *allow* termination of therapy based on non-payment of fees, as long as the client is not in immediate danger, their financial responsibilities were made clear to them, and the impact of nonpayment has been discussed. When a CSW is unable or unwilling, for any reason, to provide continued care to a client, the CSW must assist the client in making appropriate arrangements for continuation of treatment.

Payment for referrals K40, 115

Clinical social workers are both legally and ethically prohibited from accepting payment for referrals. This includes payment from clients as well as payments from the professional you referred the clients to (sometimes called "kickbacks"). The idea here is that referrals should be made *solely* on the basis of what is in the best interests of the client. If you are getting paid for referrals, there is at least the *appearance* of a conflict of interests, as you might make a referral based more on what will financially benefit you than on what will clinically benefit the client.

This issue has become more complex in recent years. In some communities, CSWs participate in "networking groups," which are organizations of professionals who sell a wide variety of goods and services. These professionals join the networking group for the specific purpose of referring potential customers to one another. However, because these groups often operate in a structure where members are rewarded for the referrals they generate (the reward might be the *absence* of a fee that they would otherwise have to pay to participate), CSWs in such groups risk being disciplined for violating the standards against receiving payment for referrals.

Gifts K120-121

While some professional standards have gotten stricter over time, the standards around giving and receiving gifts have actually grown more flexible. This is due largely to increased recognition of the cultural significance of gifts in many populations. Refusing a small gift may be culturally insensitive. The current NASW Code of Ethics does not mention gifts at all, though the existing standards around non-exploitation would certainly prohibit a CSW from placing their own interests above the client's in deciding whether to accept a gift. We consider the effect of giving or receiving the gift on the client, and the potential impact of the gift on the therapy process.

Giving a gift to a client, or accepting a gift from a client, does come with some risks. The client might perceive that the gift changes the nature of their relationship with you to a more personal one. They might hold an expectation that any gift should be reciprocated. They might expect preferential treatment in scheduling or other elements of therapy. In each of these instances (and surely many others you could come up with), the integrity of the therapeutic process can be impacted. Whether you accept or reject a client gift, it is good practice to document your decision-making on the issue. You might consider factors like the cost, nature, and meaning of the gift, how it fits within cultural norms, and its potential impact on therapy.

Third-party reimbursement K37-38, 91-94, 119

Third-party reimbursement rules. Health insurance coverage has expanded significantly since the passage of the Affordable Care Act. Of course, insurance is not the only form of third-party payment; employers, courts, nonprofit organizations, family members, and others may be the ones who are actually paying for client care. CSWs need to be aware of the rules surrounding third-party payment, including the limits on information that can be shared with third-party payers.

Some of the key legal rules regarding third-party payment include:

- **Freedom of choice.** Insurance companies typically must reimburse CSWs alongside other mental health providers. Associates do not have to be reimbursed, though some plans will pay for services provided by associates.
- **Mental disorder only.** Most insurers will only reimburse when there is a diagnosed mental disorder. Some will cover services like couple therapy when there is no diagnosis, but plans are not legally required to do so.[16]
- **Protests and complaints.** Providers can (and generally should) appeal denials of reimbursement. Consumers and providers both can complain to the state about insurance company practices. Depending on the plan, it may be governed by the state Department of Insurance or the Department of Managed Health Care.

One of the most important legal rules regarding third-party reimbursement is the legal prohibition against insurance fraud, which can draw criminal and civil penalties in addition to action against your license. Any falsification of diagnosis, procedure code, amount paid, or any other information for the purpose of receiving insurance payment is insurance fraud.

Parity laws. State and federal law require parity in insurance coverage for mental health. What this means is that insurers cannot use a different deductible or other forms of treatment limitations for mental health that they do not apply to other medical coverage. Co-payments, deductibles, and treatment limitations (like caps on the number of visits or days of coverage) for mental health must be equal to or better than the limits placed on other medical coverage.

Advocacy with third-party payers. Some clients are more able than others to navigate the complex bureaucracy of their insurance company. CSWs can assess client capacity (given their current symptoms, stressors, and abilities), challenge denials of coverage or denials of payment, and may be able to assist clients in gathering needed information about their coverage or reimbursement processes.

Ethical standards. Insurance fraud is a legal issue. At the same time, CSWs are also ethically obligated to be truthful and accurate in documentation submitted to third-party payers. Additional ethical rules that can be applied to CSWs' interactions with third-party payers include:

- Do not "participate in, condone, or be associated with dishonesty, fraud, or deception"[17]
- Ensure that billing practices accurately reflect the services provided, including the identity of service providers
- Do not disclose confidential information to payers without a specific release to do so
- Inform clients of limits to services imposed by third-party payers

Other standards applying to interactions with other service delivery systems include:

- Protect confidentiality unless authorized to share information
- Do not give or receive payment for referrals
- Ensure an orderly transfer of responsibility for the client
- Discuss whether consultation with prior providers is warranted

Advertising K39, 102-104

Advertising laws. Essentially any public statement where you suggest that you offer therapy or counseling services to the public would be considered an advertisement – the law is purposefully broad on that. The only exception in the law is for bulletins within a religious setting, published only to members of that religious group.

State law is highly specific on the **licensure status** disclosures that need to be included in *any* advertisement of a CSW's services. A licensed CSW needs to include their name, their license number, and their title ("licensed clinical social worker") or an acceptable abbreviation ("LCSW"). An associate needs to include their name, their registration number, their employer's name, an indication that they are under licensed supervision, and their title ("Registered Associate Clinical Social Worker"). That title can be abbreviated "Registered Associate CSW."

CSWs and associates can advertise themselves as **psychotherapists** and say that they perform psychotherapy, as long as they clearly list their licensure type, something the law already requires anyway.

Therapists can advertise using **fictitious business names**, so long as those names are not misleading and clients are informed of the business owners' names and licensure status before treatment begins.

Ads making any kind of **scientific claims** must be backed by published, peer-reviewed research literature.

Any **fees** included in an advertisement must be exact; you cannot advertise fees in ways like "$95 and up." For this reason, many therapists and clinics choose not to list their fees in their advertising.

It would be unprofessional conduct for any CSW to advertise in a manner that is **false, misleading, or deceptive**. Any claims that would be likely to create unjustified expectations of treatment success are also prohibited by law.

Accurate representation. Ethically, you can only advertise those degrees or credentials you have actually earned, and which are relevant to the practice of clinical social work. If you have a master's degree in social work and a doctorate in English, you could not include your doctorate as a professional qualification. Even though you do have a doctorate, it would be a misrepresentation of the credentials you hold relative to your clinical work.

Similarly, any other professional qualifications or competencies that you advertise must be accurate. If others misrepresent your qualifications or credentials, you should take reasonable steps to correct the information.

Testimonials. The NASW Code of Ethics prohibits seeking testimonials from current clients or anyone else who might be subject to undue influence. Clients and others may feel pressured by such requests. This issue has gotten more complicated in the age of Yelp, Angie's List, HealthGrades, and similar web sites designed for patients to share their experiences with a variety of professionals. Clients sometimes provide testimonials on such sites without being prompted to by therapists. CSWs should be aware that *responding* to any online testimonial may be considered a breach of client confidentiality, even when the client is openly discussing their treatment.

Affiliations. As you would expect, CSWs cannot advertise themselves as being employees, partners or associates of a group that they don't actually belong to. Any representation of professional affiliations must be accurate.

Sample Questions *See page 124 for answers and rationales*

1. A social worker learns that a family for whom she has been providing therapy is struggling to afford food. The social worker's services are being paid for by the county. The social worker is concerned about the potential impacts on the health of the children, ages 7 and 4, if the family continues to struggle to afford food. How can the social worker assist this family in keeping with her ethical responsibilities?

    a. Give the family a few dollars of her own money at each session, so the family can afford food.
    b. Offer referrals to food and financial assistance programs.
    c. Report the family for suspicion of child neglect, so that additional medical and nutritional services will be provided.
    d. Discontinue services, and "hire" one or more family members to do light work in exchange for food or money.

2. A clinical social worker in a cash-pay private practice notices that several clients have unpaid balances. Some of those with unpaid balances attend the same religious service as the CSW. As the CSW considers how to resolve the unpaid balances, how can the CSW best address their legal responsibilities?

    a. Forgive the balances of those in the religious group, and consider it a donation to that group.
    b. Terminate the clients with unpaid balances above $250, refusing to release records or provide other documentation or referrals until the balance is paid.
    c. Work with each client with an unpaid balance to develop a payment plan.
    d. Charge fees for unpaid balances, to discourage clients from carrying balances in the future. Inform all clients of the new fee and how much, if any, they additionally owe.

3. A clinical social worker with a new private practice is considering how to market their practice. He wants to operate on a sliding fee scale based on client income. How can he best fulfill his legal and ethical responsibilities?

   a. Develop a fee structure that is based on services provided, and not client income. Fee scales based on client income are prohibited in private practice settings.
   b. Advertise that services are offered "as low as" the lowest fee on his scale.
   c. Make no mention of fees in his advertising.
   d. Make his sliding fee scale a percentage of income, regardless of the income level.

Non-therapist roles

Therapy isn't the only thing that CSWs do. Far from it. Social workers also supervise, conduct research, testify in court, teach, administer clinical programs, serve as advocates, and engage in a variety of other professional activities. These activities allow you to use your clinical knowledge to benefit students, supervisees, and the general public in a variety of contexts, but they also come with potential problems, especially when you are providing non-therapy services to people who are also therapy clients.

Multiple Relationships K52-56

A multiple relationship (or "dual relationship" -- the terms are used here interchangeably) occurs any time a CSW has a relationship with a client that is separate from being their therapist. Not all multiple relationships are unethical or illegal, and some can't be avoided, especially in rural areas or in work with more tight-knit communities. The NASW Code of Ethics clarifies that multiple relationships do not have to be simultaneous – a multiple relationship can still occur (and can still be problematic) when one type of relationship begins after the other has concluded.

Assessing multiple relationships. Not all multiple relationships can be avoided, especially if you are working in a rural area or with a highly-specific population. It is also true that not all multiple relationships are problematic. If a colleague tells you that you can't see a client because "that would be a dual relationship," they haven't adequately made their case.

Multiple relationships must be carefully examined to see whether they would **impair clinical judgment** or create **risk of client exploitation**. These two considerations are critical to determining whether a multiple relationship can be allowed. If you know and like someone in your community and they ask to see you in therapy, your liking of them would surely influence how you observe them clinically -- in other words, your pre-existing view of them would impair your clinical judgment. (Impairment can mean positive bias as well as negative.) Having a client who coaches your daughter's soccer team could create risk of exploitation, as you could use your knowledge of the client's personal secrets to push for more playing time for your daughter. The fact that you wouldn't actually do this does not eliminate the risk of it, nor does it take away your responsibility to protect clients from that risk.

Even when such risks exist, though, in some cases it may be appropriate to continue with the therapy. If you are the only provider in a rural area, for example, the best interests of the client might be better served by going ahead with therapy. You would then need to take specific actions to reduce the risk of impaired judgment or exploitation.

Prohibited multiple relationships. Sexual or romantic relationships with clients and those close to the client are expressly prohibited, and discussed in greater detail below. Social workers are also ethically prohibited from taking advantage of any professional relationship to further the social worker's personal, religious, political, or business interests.

Managing boundaries. CSWs commonly take steps to ensure the integrity and boundaries of the therapy relationship. This can be especially important when it appears that a client is becoming confused about the nature of the relationship, or is wanting more of a personal or social relationship than what therapy allows.

Some examples of methods for managing boundaries include having a conversation with the client to remind them of the boundaries of therapy; maintaining a clear treatment plan with identified therapy goals; making sure all contact between client and therapist stays focused on therapeutic issues; starting and ending sessions on time; and, when clinically appropriate, limiting contact by phone or other means between scheduled session times.

Potential conflicts of interest. CSWs are ethically obligated to be alert to potential conflicts of interest as they arise. A potential conflict emerges any time a therapist engages in a non-therapist role, such as consultation, coaching, or behavior analysis, with people who are or have been clients in therapy. A potential conflict also emerges any time an outside interest may interfere with the CSW's ability to exercise impartial professional judgment.

In any instance of potential conflict of interests, CSWs have an obligation to clarify their roles, and to distinguish how any applicable non-therapist role is different from therapy. In order to avoid any risk to clients, it may be preferable to refer out for additional services that are different from those for which the CSW was initially hired.

Potentially damaging relationships. Sexual relationships, which are discussed at greater length below, are the best example of a relationship that can be damaging to the client. However, they are not the only example. Other forms of multiple relationships can harm clients directly, through poor care or exploitation, or they may harm clients more indirectly, by reducing their overall confidence in therapy as an effective and worthwhile treatment. Social relationships between CSWs and clients can create confusion about the therapist's role, for example, and can hinder success in therapy by clouding the CSW's clinical judgment.

When multiple relationships can't be avoided. Some multiple relationships are unavoidable. For example, some level of multiple relationship is created any time a CSW gets a new client through a referral from an existing client. Another example occurs in a rural area, where a CSW may have regular interaction with many clients at community gatherings. In these and similar situations, the NASW Code of Ethics requires CSWs to "take steps to protect clients and [be] responsible for setting clear, appropriate, and culturally sensitive boundaries."[18]

In some cases, the precautions may be as simple as having a conversation with the client to reassure them of confidentiality and clearly separate roles. In other cases, more stringent precautions may be appropriate, like the CSW regularly consulting on the case with a colleague.

Sexual relationships K32-33, 57-59

Risk of exploitation. The rules prohibiting sexual contact between social workers and their clients come from a fundamental understanding that because the CSW has power in the social work relationship, because clients are often emotionally vulnerable, and because the social work process happens behind closed doors, sexual relationships between CSWs and clients are likely to be exploitive and ultimately harmful to clients.

This exploitation does not require sexual *intercourse*, and the legal and ethical standards around sexual relationships are worded in such a way as to include romantically intimate relationships generally, even if there has not been intercourse. A therapist could not avoid discipline by simply telling their licensing board, "But we didn't actually have sex!"

Intimacy between therapist and client. Sexual conduct -- again, a purposefully broader term than intercourse -- between therapist and client is specifically prohibited under California law. Such contact is also specifically prohibited by both the NASW Code of Ethics, which uses the term "sexual activities or sexual contact."

Intimacy between therapist and *former* client. For former clients, state law prohibits sexual relationships for two years after the last professional contact. Even after that time, however, the NASW Code continues to strongly discourage sexual relationships with former clients, due to the risk that they will be exploitive and harmful to the former client.

Intimacy between therapist and client's spouse, partner, or family member. State laws about sexual relationships with clients and former clients apply only to the clients themselves. Under ethical guidelines, the prohibition is broader: Social workers *also* may not enter into sexually intimate relationships with client's relatives, or with *anyone else who has a close personal relationship* with the client. The NASW code goes on to clarify that it is fully the social worker's responsibility to set these boundaries, even if the other person may be consenting.

The *Professional Therapy Never Includes Sex* brochure. If your client informs you that they have had a sexual relationship with another therapist, you are required by law to provide for them the state-authored brochure *Professional Therapy Never Includes Sex*. Failure to provide the brochure is considered unprofessional conduct. Many therapists keep a copy or two of the brochure readily available in their offices; it also can be downloaded and printed when you need it.

Therapy with former romantic partners. Just as it would be unethical to start having sex with a former client (subject to the rules noted above), it would also be unethical to accept a client in therapy who was a former sexual partner. This type of multiple relationship is expressly prohibited by the NASW Code of Ethics. Entering into a therapy relationship with the partner or immediate family member of someone with whom the therapist has had a prior sexual relationship is not directly prohibited by the NASW code, but would still likely be addressed by the standards surrounding multiple relationships.

Research ethics K122-125

Procedures for safeguarding research participants. The most important safeguard for research participants is the process of informed consent. Just as a client should be fully informed of the processes, risks, and potential benefits of therapy, a research participant should be fully informed of the processes, risks, and benefits of their participation in a study. Most studies are overseen by some form of Institutional Review Board, which reviews the protocols and protections the researchers have in place.

Necessary disclosures to research participants. Under the NASW Code of Ethics, research participants need to be informed of potential risks and benefits from participating. They should also be clearly informed of what participation entails: What is being asked of them, and for how long? Participants should be informed of the limits to confidentiality that apply to their participation, the steps being taken to preserve their confidentiality, and how long records of the research will be retained before being destroyed. Finally, participants must be informed that they can withdraw their consent and end participation at any time, without penalty.

Some forms of research, like naturalistic observation or archival research, do not involve informed consent processes. The NASW code notes that these methods should only be employed without informed consent when "a rigorous and responsible review" has found the research worthwhile, and when alternatives that involve informed consent are not feasible.

Client rights when participating in research. In addition to the right to be informed about the research they are participating in, clients also have the right to decline or withdraw their participation in a study at any time. They have a right to confidentiality unless they sign a waiver specifically authorizing the release of information from their participation. (If the study is a study involving therapy services, the same limits of confidentiality would apply as ordinarily apply in therapy, and the clients should be informed of this as part of the informed consent process.) Under the NASW code, they have the right to be protected from unwarranted danger or distress.

Confidentiality of research data. Unless clients provide a written waiver, CSWs consider any information they learn about a research participant to be confidential, subject to the exceptions to confidentiality outlined earlier. If others may be able to gain access to a participant's research data, the CSW should explain this possibility at the beginning of the study and share their plan for protecting confidentiality.

Supervision K128

Supervisors have a number of specific responsibilities defined in the NASW Code of Ethics. In brief, supervisors are required to:

- Have the necessary skills and knowledge to supervise, getting consultation when needed
- Set clear, appropriate, and culturally sensitive boundaries
- Avoid multiple relationships where there is risk of impaired judgment or exploitation
- Evaluate supervisee performance in a manner that is fair, respectful, and based on clearly established criteria
- Ensure clients are aware when services are being provided by students (this ethical standard applies to fieldwork instructors)

Legal and other professional roles K109-110

Responsibility to clarify role. CSWs often serve in professional capacities that are different from being a therapist or supervisor. For example, CSWs may serve as custody evaluators, expert witnesses, consultants, or in other roles. When doing so, it is important that CSWs be clear (with everyone: themselves, clients, courts, and anyone else involved) about what their role is, how it is different from therapy or other services, and how client information may be used and shared with the court or with others.

Dual or conflicting roles. CSWs are responsible for clearly identifying their roles and minimizing conflicts of interest. A common example (one specifically noted in the NASW Code of Ethics) involves a social worker being asked to testify in a child custody dispute involving clients. In the therapist role, a CSW is working clinically with clients to help them achieve therapeutic goals. This can involve actively soliciting information about the clients' parenting struggles, interpersonal conflicts, substance use, and other information that may place clients in a vulnerable position. In an evaluator role, the CSW is to remain objective, simply assessing an individual or family's functioning. The information a client provides to a CSW in a treatment role may actively work against that client's interests if the CSW then testifies to that information in a custody hearing.

A CSW who has proper releases of information can inform the court of a minor's or family's progress in therapy while remaining outside of an evaluator role. The CSW would just need to be very careful to not include statements that might be considered as evaluative statements related to custody, visitation, or whatever legal proceeding is underway.

Another common role conflict for CSWs comes in administering agencies or programs where other CSWs are providing clinical services. CSWs in administrative roles have additional responsibilities under the NASW code, several of which surround fair processes for employment and evaluation. CSWs must manage boundaries and clarify roles well if, for example, they are providing clinical supervision to someone for whom the CSW also provides evaluation for employment. Without role clarity, the supervisee may rightly wonder whether it is in their interest to be fully transparent in supervision about any problems with current cases.

When a CSW is engaged in dual or conflicting roles, the CSW is ethically obligated to inform clients and to take steps to resolve the issue in a way that protects client interests. In some instances, referring out for one or both of these roles may be the best resolution.

Sample Questions *See page 127 for answers and rationales*

1. An LCSW is conducting research at a university on the long-term effects of child sexual abuse. He has several clients in his private practice who were abused as children, and he hopes to encourage them to serve as participants in his study. Participation involves a series of structured interviews in which the participant is asked to go into significant detail about the abuse they experienced, their family's reaction when first told, and the long-term impacts on the participant's life. Ethically, the best option for the LCSW is to:

   a. Motivate participation in the study by offering clients three free sessions of therapy if they participate in the research study.
   b. Motivate participation in the study by informing clients that the study's interviews will not be emotionally difficult, and will only cover information they have already discussed in session.
   c. Motivate participation in the study by informing clients of the potential benefits of the study for others who experienced abuse.
   d. Motivate participation in the study by temporarily discontinuing the therapy and using the study interviews, for which the client is not charged, as replacement "sessions."

2. A clinical social worker is at a concert, and sees a teenage client at the concert with a friend. The client and the friend both appear to be intoxicated. At one point toward the end of the concert, the client notices the CSW, and quickly puts her head down in embarrassment. How should the CSW address their ethical responsibilities?

   a. Walk up to the client, without revealing their relationship, and say something along the lines of, "You're allowed to have fun." At the next scheduled session, pretend she did not see the client at all.
   b. Leave the concert, and consider terminating therapy as the integrity of the therapeutic relationship has been corrupted. The therapist's judgment is no longer based solely on clinical information.
   c. Stay at the concert, avoid further contact with the client, and inform the client's parents of what the CSW observed.
   d. Stay at the concert, and allow the client to determine whether they will say hello. Discuss therapeutic boundaries at the next session.

Unprofessional conduct

When a therapist violates professional standards, they are said to have committed unprofessional conduct. The BBS exists to protect the public, not the professionals, and will investigate and (if appropriate) punish unprofessional conduct when it is reported.

Unprofessional conduct laws K35

State law currently defines 28 specific categories of unprofessional conduct.[19] For our purposes, it's most important to know what unprofessional conduct *means*: It refers to **actions taken in a professional role that are below minimum professional standards.** Unlike criminal cases (where you could go to jail) or civil cases (where you might have to pay damages to someone you have wronged), unprofessional conduct rules apply to your professional role. "Unprofessional conduct" refers to those behaviors that can result in action being taken against your license or registration.

The types of conduct defined in state law as unprofessional conduct include the following. The language here is lightly edited from state law, and grouped into categories:

Sexual misconduct
    Sexual contact with a client or former client
    Committing a sex crime with a minor
    Committing a sex crime
    Sexual misconduct
    Failure to provide *Professional Therapy Never Includes Sex*

Scope of practice and competence
    Performing or offering services outside of scope

Impairment
    Impairment due to mental or physical illness or drug dependence
    Drug dependence or use with a client while providing services

Confidentiality
    Failure to maintain confidentiality

Crimes and bad acts
    Conviction of a crime
    Committing a dishonest, corrupt, or fraudulent act
    Discipline by another board or by another state

Fraud
    Getting or attempting to get a license by fraud
    Misrepresenting your license or qualifications
    Impersonating a licensee
    Aiding someone else's unlicensed activity

Testing
    Violating exam security or integrity

Supervision
    Improper supervision of a trainee or associate
    Violations during or involving required hours of experience

Fees and advertising
    Failure to disclose fees in advance
    False, misleading, deceptive, or improper advertising
    Paying, accepting, or soliciting a fee for referrals

Record-keeping
    Failure to keep records consistent with sound clinical judgment
    Failure to comply with client requests for access to records

Telemedicine
    Violating state telehealth standards

General misconduct
    General unprofessional conduct
    Gross negligence or incompetence
    Intentionally or recklessly causing physical or emotional harm

Preparing for the 2019 California Clinical Social Work Law & Ethics Exam

The category simply called "general unprofessional conduct" allows the BBS to act against you if you violate other law, professional ethical codes, or the professional standard of care while in your professional role. In this way, behaviors that are unethical can also be considered illegal, even if they aren't specifically designated as such in the law.

Now, **you don't need to memorize the entire list above.** Most of it, again, is simply what you would expect (and what is covered in this book). Knowing all of the categories will not be nearly as helpful to you as being able to determine whether a particular behavior qualifies as unprofessional conduct under the law.

When a therapist engages in unprofessional conduct, the client may submit a complaint to the BBS. The BBS then has an investigations unit that assesses the complaint, determines whether it is actionable, and investigates if appropriate. During this time, the CSW has the opportunity to defend themselves. If the CSW is found to have committed unprofessional conduct, the BBS can levy fines, place the CSW's license (or registration, in cases involving CSW associates) on suspension or probation, restrict their practice, and in severe cases, revoke the CSW's license or registration. They also may require other actions, such as regular drug testing, while the CSW is on probation or in order to resolve the disciplinary issue.[20] The disciplinary process is meaningfully different from a criminal trial or a civil lawsuit; the BBS only needs to find *clear and convincing evidence* that a violation occurred to issue a penalty.

Unethical or incompetent colleagues K126-127

CSWs not only need to be able to recognize when their own ability to provide therapy is compromised. You also must be aware of times when a *colleague's* ability to provide ethical and effective therapy is compromised. **Situations that can impair the integrity or effectiveness of therapy** include multiple relationships (subject to the boundaries previously described); therapist substance abuse, mental illness, or emotional disturbance; bias or discrimination by the therapist; exploitation; and many more.

Unlike some other states, **California does not have any rules allowing clinical social workers to directly report colleagues who are behaving in unethical or incompetent ways.** So when a client tells you about bad behavior on the part of their previous therapist, you are required to keep this information confidential. Reporting it to the board yourself, or directly confronting the colleague, would be an illegal breach of confidentiality. If a client grants permission for you to talk with the other therapist (through a written release of information), you could then address the other therapist, but it would be important to avoid taking the client's report at face value. There are often two very different sides to such stories, and social workers treat each other with respect.[21]

If you learn of another therapist's unethical or incompetent behavior *directly from that therapist*, you may have more options. For example, if you learn that a colleague in your clinic is struggling with an alcohol abuse problem, you could encourage your colleague to seek treatment and to discontinue seeing clients until the problem is under control. The NASW Code of Ethics encourages CSWs to **offer assistance to colleagues who are impaired** and need to take remedial action.[22] Doing so would certainly be in the best interests of their clients. If the other therapist refuses, you must carefully balance competing standards. The NASW Code of Ethics generally requires social workers avoid unwarranted criticism of colleagues.[23] At the same time, the code demands that social workers who become aware of a colleague's impaired, unethical, or incompetent behavior attempt to consult with and assist that colleague (subject to the legal limitations surrounding confidentiality noted above).[24] If those efforts fail, you should take action through appropriate channels, if it is feasible to do so.

There is one situation that legally *requires* specific action on your part based on another therapist's incompetence: When there has been **a sexual relationship between that therapist and their client**. If your current client tells you that they had a sexual relationship with their prior therapist, you are legally required to provide the client with the state-authored brochure called *Professional Therapy Never Includes Sex*. Failure to do so is unprofessional conduct, as noted above. Even when you're supplying this brochure, though, you cannot report the other therapist's conduct to the board without client permission. You can, however, encourage your client to do so. This route is preferable, as the investigating board would need to follow up with the client directly to obtain additional information and get their permission to obtain treatment records from the prior therapist.

What is most important in a situation like this is that you take appropriate action to promote the welfare of clients. While confidentiality laws may prevent you from reporting it yourself when a client tells you that another therapist is behaving unethically or incompetently, you can (and often should) encourage the client to report that behavior themselves. You can't *require* the client to make that report – that would be putting your wishes above the client's – but you can encourage it.

What You Need to Know

Sample Question *See page 130 for answer and rationale*

1. A client tells you that she left her previous therapist after the therapist became erratic and unfocused. The therapist's father died six months ago, and the client wonders whether the therapist had been drinking to cope with the loss. The client's previous therapist is also a clinical social worker, and is someone you know personally. You should:

   a. Apologize on behalf of your colleague. Report the previous therapist to the BBS, as she appears to be unable to provide quality clinical care.
   b. Without disclosing what the client said, reach out to your colleague and offer to provide confidential therapy to the colleague to protect her clients.
   c. Without disclosing what the client said, check in with the colleague. If she volunteers any information about her grief process, encourage the colleague to enter treatment.
   d. Directly confront the colleague with what you know. Inform the colleague's employer that she may not be healthy enough to provide services.

Sample Questions: Answers and Rationales

Parameters of practice (p. 45)

1. A client sees an LCSW at a local community clinic for court-mandated anger management groups. The client comes to dislike the LCSW and becomes disruptive, frequently comparing the group to jail, and saying "I'm not free when I'm here." In considering her ethical responsibilities, the LCSW should:

   a. **Incorrect.** Empathize and validate the client's feeling of disempowerment.
   b. **Incorrect.** Terminate therapy with the client and refer them back to court.
   c. **CORRECT.** Remind the client that he is free to attend any anger management group he wishes, or none at all.
   d. **Incorrect.** Threaten to inform the court of his statements if he continues, and encourage him to become more open to the group process.

Empathy and validation (A) may be clinically appropriate but do not address any legal or ethical responsibilities. Termination (B) is premature, given that client frustration with mandated treatment is relatively normal and often can be resolved. While repeated disclosures of the limits of confidentiality are encouraged, using those limits as threats (D) undermines efforts to work collaboratively with the court system. Option C supports client autonomy and maximizes client choice. While failure to attend groups may have legal consequences for the client, they do have the right to make that choice. The client can attend any group, or none; the social worker is not holding the client against their will.

Sample Questions: Answers and Rationales

2. A 14-year-old client consented to her own treatment at a nonprofit agency, which agreed to treat her for $5/session. The client tells the therapist (a CSW) that the client has been abusing a friend's prescription painkillers. Legally, the CSW should:

   a. **Incorrect.** Notify the local child protective service agency.
   b. **Incorrect.** Notify the client's parent or guardian, as the behavior is considered high-risk.
   c. **Incorrect.** Work with the client to develop a plan to gradually reduce dosage and ultimately stop the client's drug use.
   d. **CORRECT.** Document the discussion and refer the client to a physician.

Drug use, in and of itself, is not considered child abuse (a). No such report is needed. Since the client consented to treatment on their own, the parents do not have a right to the client's records; even a high-risk behavior would not be disclosed (b) unless doing so was to prevent imminent danger. Advising the client on reducing prescription drug dosage would be considered giving medical advice and is out of an CSW's scope of practice. A referral to a physician (d) is appropriate.

Documentation and disclosures (p. 56)

1. A clinical social worker receives a request from a former client for their complete therapy records. The client's treatment occurred four years ago. When the CSW locates the former client's file, the CSW finds that the file is disorganized, and consists mostly of brief, handwritten notes. The CSW, whose current record-keeping is much improved, is embarrassed by the state of this old file. How should the CSW address their legal responsibilities in this case?

   a. **Incorrect.** Only agree to provide the client a written treatment summary in lieu of the full record.
   b. **Incorrect.** Recreate the handwritten notes in a more structured, typed format, adding details as needed. Discard the handwritten notes and provide the updated record within 10 days of the client's request.
   c. **Incorrect.** Refuse to release the file, on the grounds that it may be damaging to the CSW's relationship with the former client.
   d. **CORRECT.** Release the file in its current form, and offer to address any questions the former client may have.

While treatment summaries (A) are often preferable responses to requests for client records, in this case the client specifically requested their *complete* record. With some limitations, they have a legal right to that record. Altering the record and presenting it as if it were the original record (B) could be considered fraud. While CSWs can refuse to release records if they believe doing so would harm the client, there's nothing in the question to suggest such risk of harm. The CSW's embarrassment is not adequate justification to refuse a record request (C). The CSW is obligated to release the file. Offering to address any questions is not a legal obligation, but may alleviate any confusion on the part of the client.

Sample Questions: Answers and Rationales

2. A client asks whether her 75-year-old mother can be part of her therapy. The mother speaks English, but can only read and write in her native language, which you as the therapist are not familiar with. You believe that including the mother in the therapy may be helpful to the client. You should:

   a. **Incorrect.** Have the mother sign your informed consent form and join the therapy.
   b. **CORRECT.** Verbally discuss the process, risks, and benefits of therapy with the mother to help her decide whether to join the therapy, and document the discussion and her response.
   c. **Incorrect.** Refer the mother to a therapist who speaks her native language, and ask the client to sign a Release of Information form authorizing you to speak to that therapist.
   d. **Incorrect.** Ask the mother to teach you her native language so that you can provide all appropriate paperwork in her language.

The correct answer is B. Consent for therapy should be documented, but the client's consent does not need to be in writing. Such a requirement would make it impossible to work with clients who are illiterate. A verbal conversation is the best way to ensure that the mother is truly able to exercise her autonomy and provide informed consent for treatment. A is incorrect because the mother's signature would not mean much on a form she could not understand. C is incorrect because it would not fulfill the request of the client, to have the mother be part of the client's therapy, which you also believe may be helpful. D is incorrect because this would be both time-consuming and a potentially inappropriate dual relationship.

Preparing for the 2019 California Clinical Social Work Law & Ethics Exam

Confidentiality and privilege
(p. 73)

1. An elder client tells a CSW working in hospice care that the client was recently taken to a local religious gathering against her will by her 50-year-old daughter. The daughter is a member of the religious group. By the client's report, the daughter told her mother that "this might be good for you, being around people with good values" and did not bring the mother home when the mother said she was uncomfortable there. Furthermore, the daughter donated the cash in the client's purse to the religious group, despite the client's repeated statements to her daughter that the client did not support the group. How should the CSW respond to their legal obligations in this case?

    a. **Incorrect.** Report suspected elder abuse (specifically, kidnapping)
    b. **CORRECT.** Report suspected elder abuse (specifically, financial abuse)
    c. **Incorrect.** Report suspected elder abuse (specifically, emotional abuse)
    d. **Incorrect.** Report suspected elder abuse (specifically, isolation)

    All four options share reporting, so it is safe to presume that reporting is a requirement here. The differences relate to the *type* of abuse being reported. The law surrounding kidnapping (a) requires that the elder have been taken across state lines, which is not stated in the question. Emotional abuse (c) is not a specific category of elder abuse in statute, though the elder abuse rules do provide wide latitude for therapists to report anything they find to be abusive to an elder. Isolation (d) is perhaps most clearly not appropriate here, as the daughter took the client to a social event. Financial abuse (b) is most appropriate here, given that the client states her daughter took her money against her will and spent it on a cause she would not have supported on her own.

Sample Questions: Answers and Rationales

2. A 15-year-old girl is seeing a CSW individually for issues related to body image and self-esteem. Her parents provided consent for the therapy and pay for her sessions, but do not participate. The girl tells the CSW that she has been exploring her sexuality. While her parents were out of town, she had sexual intercourse with a friend's 19-year-old brother. A few days later, she had intercourse with another boy, an 18-year-old senior at her high school. The CSW should manage their legal responsibilities by:

   a. **Incorrect.** Reporting child abuse to the local child protective service agency
   b. **Incorrect.** Investigating to ensure that the sexual activity was not coerced or while under the influence of drugs or alcohol
   c. **Incorrect.** Notifying the parents of their daughter's high-risk sexual behavior
   d. **CORRECT.** Maintaining confidentiality

The age combination of the partners, in both instances of sexual activity, does not require reporting (a). If either boy were 21 or over, or under 14, these combinations would be reportable. While it may be clinically relevant to explore the context of the sexual activity in more detail, the CSW is not obligated to do so, and in fact should not position themselves as an investigator (b). While the parents may be able to access their daughter's treatment records, the CSW does not have a responsibility to proactively inform them of sexual behavior; further, there is nothing in the question that would necessarily classify this girl's behavior as "high-risk" (c). In the absence of a legal requirement or allowance for disclosure, the CSW is legally obligated to maintain confidentiality.

Preparing for the 2019 California Clinical Social Work Law & Ethics Exam

3. The client of a CSW is on trial for fraud. The client is accused of submitting false claims to the client's insurance company, including claims for sessions that did not actually take place. At the client's request, the CSW had provided superbills and related documentation to the client to support her insurance claims, including those for sessions that did not happen. The CSW is called upon to testify under court order. How can the CSW best address their legal responsibilities in this case?

    a. **Incorrect.** Refuse to share any information on the basis of therapist-client privilege
    b. **Incorrect.** Contact the client and determine how they wish to proceed
    c. **Incorrect.** Acknowledge that the overbilling occurred, but describe it as an administrative error rather than incriminating the client
    d. **CORRECT.** Provide specific and detailed testimony about the scheme

Here, the client sought out the CSW to commit a crime -- that's clarified by "At the client's request." That is a specific exception to privilege (A), and one that we can safely assume has already been determined, based on the fact that the CSW is testifying under a court order. With such an order in place, the CSW is no longer in a position to defer to the client's wishes about testifying (B). The CSW has no obligation to lie on the client's behalf (C), and doing so would violate the general ethical principle of fidelity – in addition to being false testimony under oath, a legal violation otherwise known as perjury. At this point, the only available option to the CSW is to testify truthfully as to what happened. (You could, of course, entertain a side debate about whether the therapist should refuse to testify on the grounds of self-incrimination, otherwise known as pleading the Fifth Amendment. But that's not offered as an option here.)

Sample Questions: Answers and Rationales

Treatment (p. 86)

1. A client has cancelled three of the last seven scheduled sessions with an LCSW, and been a no-show for the other four. Each time, the client has promised to pay any balance charged, and to come in for a session the following week. The LCSW finds herself irritated with the client's behavior, going so far as to warn the client two weeks ago that she would simply close the client's case and refer out if the client didn't come in. The client was a no-show for the next two scheduled sessions. Even before this long series of missed appointments, the LCSW found herself personally disliking the client. How should the LCSW manage her ethical responsibilities in this case?

   a. **Incorrect.** Meaningfully assess for crisis, and continue as the client's treatment provider if necessary.
   b. **CORRECT.** Close the case, providing the client with appropriate referrals to other providers.
   c. **Incorrect.** Provide the client at least two additional warnings, one of which must be in writing, prior to terminating therapy.
   d. **Incorrect.** Seek consultation to address countertransference, and continue to work toward the client more regularly attending therapy.

You can terminate therapy for almost any reason, so long as that reason is not discriminatory in nature, any evident crisis issues are addressed, and the client is provided with appropriate referrals. In this case, the client has a pattern of non-attendance and was warned that this would lead to termination. There is no legal or ethical responsibility to provide redundant warnings (C). While assessing for crisis is generally a good idea (A), even if crisis issues were present, this would not necessarily obligate the therapist to remain the client's treatment provider. If anything, evidence of crisis combined with non-attendance in therapy might suggest a need for coordinated transfer to a higher level of care. While the CSW's response to the client may indeed indicate countertransference (D), therapists are not required to continue working with clients they don't like. Termination is appropriate here.

Preparing for the 2019 California Clinical Social Work Law & Ethics Exam

2. As a client leaves a CSW's office, the CSW believes the client poses a serious danger to the client's spouse. (The client had been making threats in session about what he would do to her.) The CSW, knowing the couple lives roughly 30 minutes from the CSW's office, calls the client immediately, and is able to resolve the danger. The client disavows any continued plan to harm his spouse, and apologizes to the CSW for "getting so out of hand." What does the CSW need to do to resolve the CSW's legal responsibility?

    a. **Incorrect.** Notify the spouse and law enforcement immediately
    b. **Incorrect.** Notify the spouse immediately
    c. **CORRECT.** Notify law enforcement within 24 hours
    d. **Incorrect.** Notify the local child protective services agency

While warning an intended victim in a *Tarasoff* situation grants the CSW certain additional legal protections, it is not always necessary or appropriate to do so. In this case, the CSW was able to fully resolve the threat on their own, before notifying the intended victim or law enforcement. Still, under state law, the fact that the CSW's *Tarasoff* responsibilities were triggered *at all* means that the CSW must report the threatening person to law enforcement within 24 hours, even if notifying law enforcement was not necessary to resolve the initial threat. As noted in the study guide, the idea of this law is to prevent potentially dangerous individuals from buying guns.

Sample Questions: Answers and Rationales

3. A clinical social worker is working with a same-sex couple in therapy. One partner expresses that he is feeling hostile toward the CSW. The CSW asks to meet briefly with that partner alone. During the individual discussion, the partner says that he feels the CSW is siding against him, interrupting him, and generally not respecting his complaints about the relationship. The CSW is surprised by this, and begins to wonder what else the CSW has been missing in session. How should the CSW handle their responsibilities in this case?

    a. **Incorrect.** Recognize each individual as a unique client, and offer to see the partners individually if they prefer.

    b. **Incorrect.** Discontinue treatment, as the therapeutic relationship has been corrupted, and refer to at least three therapists competent in working with same-sex couples.

    c. **Incorrect.** Conceptualize the client's reaction as paranoia, as it is inconsistent with the therapist's experience. Integrate this into the CSW's understanding of the dynamics of the relationship.

    d. **CORRECT.** Work to restore the therapeutic relationship with the partner, and consider finding consultation or supervision for this case.

Maintaining the therapeutic relationship becomes a complex task with couples and families. Here, the CSW is surprised by a partner feeling ganged up on. The CSW should not respond by defensively discontinuing treatment (B) or dismissing the client's experience as evidence of pathology (C). Since the unit of treatment is the couple, splitting them on the basis of this exchange (A) is premature at best, and raises its own set of ethical concerns. A more appropriate first step would be to resolve this rift in the therapeutic relationship without otherwise compromising the established therapeutic process.

The business of social work

(p. 95)

1. A social worker learns that a family for whom she has been providing therapy is struggling to afford food. The social worker's services are being paid for by the county. The social worker is concerned about the potential impacts on the health of the children, ages 7 and 4, if the family continues to struggle to afford food. How can the social worker assist this family in keeping with her ethical responsibilities?

   a. **Incorrect.** Give the family a few dollars of her own money at each session, so the family can afford food.
   b. **CORRECT.** Offer referrals to food and financial assistance programs.
   c. **Incorrect.** Report the family for suspicion of child neglect, so that additional medical and nutritional services will be provided.
   d. **Incorrect.** Discontinue services, and "hire" one or more family members to do light work in exchange for food or money.

Gifting clients money in this situation (A) may be generous, but also risks changing the nature of the clinical relationship, particularly when done on an ongoing basis. Reporting suspected child neglect (C) is not supported by the facts in the question; there is nothing stated that provides reasonable suspicion that neglect has occurred. Discontinuing services when the clients are in such need (D) could be considered client abandonment, and hiring one or more family members would create a problematic multiple relationship. This is especially true if the multiple relationship occurs immediately after treatment was abruptly halted. The best solution to assist the family while also preserving the integrity of the clinical relationship is to provide appropriate referrals.

Sample Questions: Answers and Rationales

2. A clinical social worker in a cash-pay private practice notices that several clients have unpaid balances. Some of those with unpaid balances attend the same religious service as the CSW. As the CSW considers how to resolve the unpaid balances, how can the CSW best address their legal responsibilities?

    a. **Incorrect.** Forgive the balances of those in the religious group, and consider it a donation to that group.
    b. **Incorrect.** Terminate the clients with unpaid balances above $250, refusing to release records or provide other documentation or referrals until the balance is paid.
    c. **CORRECT.** Work with each client with an unpaid balance to develop a payment plan.
    d. **Incorrect.** Charge fees for unpaid balances, to discourage clients from carrying balances in the future. Inform all clients of the new fee and how much, if any, they additionally owe.

Forgiving the balances of those who share the CSW's religious practice, while not forgiving the balances of others (A), would likely be considered discrimination based on religion. Terminating clients for lack of payment (B) can be ethically acceptable, but must be done in a clinically responsible way. The CSW cannot refuse to release records on the basis of an unpaid balance. While it is legal to charge fees for unpaid balances (D), such fees need to be spelled out to clients *before* they are implemented -- typically in the initial informed consent agreement. Imposing them before informing clients of them would be a violation.

3. A clinical social worker with a new private practice is considering how to market their practice. He wants to operate on a sliding fee scale based on client income. How can he best fulfill his legal and ethical responsibilities?

    a. **Incorrect.** Develop a fee structure that is based on services provided, and not client income. Fee scales based on client income are prohibited in private practice settings.
    b. **Incorrect.** Advertise that services are offered "as low as" the lowest fee on his scale.
    c. **CORRECT.** Make no mention of fees in his advertising.
    d. **Incorrect.** Make his sliding fee scale a percentage of income, regardless of the income level.

Sliding scales are allowed in private practice, making (A) incorrect. Note that some insurance carriers have terms in their contracts effectively prohibiting such scales, which makes the "cash-pay" distinction important. An "as low as" advertisement (B) is considered misleading in state law. And a scale that is a percentage of income *regardless of income level* (D) would likely be considered exploitive of high-income clients, considering the high fees that could result. Option C is the best answer here; while CSWs are allowed to state fees in their advertising, they are not required to do so. Since every other option is clearly incorrect, this approach – removing fees from advertising – is the best one of the choices available.

Sample Questions: Answers and Rationales

Non-therapist roles (p. 105)

1. An LCSW is conducting research at a university on the long-term effects of child sexual abuse. He has several clients in his private practice who were abused as children, and he hopes to encourage them to serve as participants in his study. Participation involves a series of structured interviews in which the participant is asked to go into significant detail about the abuse they experienced, their family's reaction when first told, and the long-term impacts on the participant's life. Ethically, the best option for the LCSW is to:

   a. **Incorrect.** Motivate participation in the study by offering clients three free sessions of therapy if they participate in the research study.
   b. **Incorrect.** Motivate participation in the study by informing clients that the study's interviews will not be emotionally difficult, and will only cover information they have already discussed in session.
   c. **CORRECT.** Motivate participation in the study by informing clients of the potential benefits of the study for others who experienced abuse.
   d. **Incorrect.** Motivate participation in the study by temporarily discontinuing the therapy and using the study interviews, for which the client is not charged, as replacement "sessions."

While most CSWs do not spend a great deal of time engaging in independent research, social workers are expected to be aware of basic research ethics. Here, three of the four options point to actions that specifically violate ethical standards surrounding CSW research. Offering clients free therapy sessions for their participation in the study (A) could be considered misuse of the therapeutic role; the clients' therapy should be unaffected by their choice to participate or not. Telling the clients that participation in the study "will not be emotionally difficult" (B) is a promise the therapist may not be able to keep, and thus likely crosses the line into using deception to gain participants. Summarily pausing therapy and asking the clients to use the research as therapy (D) creates an avoidable dual relationship, one that presents meaningful risk of -- and indeed, may already qualify as -- exploitation. Informing prospective participants of the risks and benefits of participating in a research project (C) is a specific ethical obligation.

Sample Questions: Answers and Rationales

2. A clinical social worker is at a concert, and sees a teenage client at the concert with a friend. The client and the friend both appear to be intoxicated. At one point toward the end of the concert, the client notices the CSW, and quickly puts her head down in embarrassment. How should the CSW address their ethical responsibilities?

   a. **Incorrect.** Walk up to the client, without revealing their relationship, and say something along the lines of, "You're allowed to have fun." At the next scheduled session, pretend she did not see the client at all.
   b. **Incorrect.** Leave the concert, and consider terminating therapy as the integrity of the therapeutic relationship has been corrupted. The therapist's judgment is no longer based solely on clinical information.
   c. **Incorrect.** Stay at the concert, avoid further contact with the client, and inform the client's parents of what the CSW observed.
   d. **CORRECT.** Stay at the concert, and allow the client to determine whether they will say hello. Discuss therapeutic boundaries at the next session.

Clients and therapists encounter each other by chance with some regularity. This is especially common in rural areas, and among some tightly-knit communities. CSWs typically address this possibility at the beginning of therapy, or in their informed consent documents. The therapist may wish to resolve the client's embarrassment by going directly to her (A), but this would likely heighten the client's embarrassment, and may require an explanation to the friend -- needlessly risking that the therapeutic relationship would be revealed. The therapist has no ethical obligation to leave the concert (B), and terminating therapy based on this chance encounter would be premature and likely inappropriate. Informing the parents of what the CSW observed (C) would be a breach of confidentiality unless such disclosures had been explicitly agreed to at the outset of therapy, something that is not indicated in the question. The most ethically sound choice is to remain at the concert without allowing it to create a dual relationship (D), and revisiting boundaries around confidentiality at the next session.

Unprofessional conduct (p. 111)

1. A client tells you that she left her previous therapist after the therapist became erratic and unfocused. The therapist's father died six months ago, and the client wonders whether the therapist had been drinking to cope with the loss. The client's previous therapist is also a clinical social worker, and is someone you know personally. You should:

   a. **Incorrect.** Apologize on behalf of your colleague. Report the previous therapist to the BBS, as she appears to be unable to provide quality clinical care.
   b. **Incorrect.** Without disclosing what the client said, reach out to your colleague and offer to provide confidential therapy to the colleague to protect her clients.
   c. **CORRECT.** Without disclosing what the client said, check in with the colleague. If she volunteers any information about her grief process, encourage the colleague to enter treatment.
   d. **Incorrect.** Directly confront the colleague with what you know. Inform the colleague's employer that she may not be healthy enough to provide services.

The correct answer is C. The NASW Code of Ethics guides CSWs to assist struggling colleagues in obtaining help for issues that interfere with clinical care. We cannot, however, share this information with the BBS or the employer – or with the colleague, for that matter – as this would be a breach of client confidentiality. Providing direct treatment to the friend would be an improper dual relationship.

Answers to Sample Questions

Batting Practice

Preparing for the 2019 California Clinical Social Work Law & Ethics Exam

A few more sample questions

The exam itself will not simply ask you to recount facts from the preceding pages. Instead, it will ask you to *apply and integrate* the legal and ethical standards that govern the field. That's why the sample questions so far have taken the form of case vignettes instead of simple memorization. Over the next few pages, you'll get some more practice.

What makes these questions a bit different (and, indeed, a bit tougher) from the ones you've seen already is that they ask you to combine multiple areas of knowledge when determining the correct answer. You may need to pull from several content areas to rule out incorrect responses and determine the correct one.

These next few questions aren't meant to be a sample test, just a handful of items to give you a sense of how knowledge might be organized and applied to arrive at the right answers here. In each question, assume you are an CSW acting within your professional role. Remember that, as is the case on the test itself, questions may be complex, and they may require careful reading – but they aren't designed to trick. There's a single, best answer for each question.

Batting Practice

1. Your client is suing her employer, saying that long hours and stressful working conditions caused her anxiety disorder. You receive a subpoena from the employer's attorney, calling on you to produce the client's records and to testify in the case. You contact your client, who asks you not to testify or share her records. You should:

   a. Advise her to drop or settle her lawsuit, since you will likely be required to testify and to share her records.
   b. Respond to the subpoena by asserting privilege.
   c. Waive privilege on the client's behalf, since an exception to privilege applies.
   d. Provide no response to the subpoena, since it did not come from a judge.

2. A client who recently moved out of state leaves her former therapist, a California CSW, a voicemail to ask that the CSW forward her file to the client's new therapist where she now lives. Considering the CSW's legal responsibilities, the CSW should:

   a. Release the file directly to the client.
   b. Contact the client and ask the client to submit a signed release authorizing the file to be sent.
   c. Contact the licensing board of the client's new home state to determine applicable laws there for disclosure of health information.
   d. Contact the client's new therapist and ask the therapist and the client to sign a release authorizing the file to be sent.

3. You are working with a Latina mother and her 7-year-old son in therapy, when you observe unusual bruises on the boy's face and arms. The bruises seem to be in several different stages of healing. When you ask how he got the bruises, both the boy and his mother refuse to answer. You should:

    a. Report suspected child abuse.
    b. Consider whether physical discipline is common in Latin cultures.
    c. Remind the mother of the limits of confidentiality.
    d. Ask the child to remove his shirt to inspect his torso for additional injuries.

4. An Associate CSW has been working under supervision in a private practice setting for two years. The Associate achieves licensure, and informs the supervisor that the Associate will be starting their own private practice. The now-former Associate would like to bring their current clients along to the new practice. How can the Associate CSW best address their ethical responsibilities?

    a. Understand that the clients are ultimately clients of the supervisor, and allow the clients to determine how they wish to proceed.
    b. Understand that the clients are ultimately clients of the supervisor, and allow the supervisor to determine which clients may follow the new licensee into their private practice.
    c. Retain the files for all clients who wish to follow the new licensee into their private practice, allowing the supervisor to make copies if the supervisor wishes.
    d. Allow the clients to determine whether to follow the new licensee into private practice, paying the supervisor a fee for each client who does so. This fee covers the supervisor's costs for marketing that brought the clients in to see the Associate originally.

5. Your client has health insurance, but the insurance carrier is refusing to cover the client's therapy because she is seeing you for couple therapy and does not, in your assessment, qualify for a diagnosis of mental illness. You should:

    a. Assess the client's ability to advocate on her own behalf with the insurance company.
    b. Offer to include an "insurance diagnosis" on the client's paperwork to facilitate coverage.
    c. Work with the client to develop an alternative plan for payment.
    d. Discontinue therapy.

6. The client of an CSW notices that before her session, as the CSW is escorting her previous appointment out of the office, the CSW and the person she is escorting out are discussing plans to have coffee together later. The client asks the CSW about this at the beginning of her session. The client tells the CSW that she, too, would like to have a more personal and social relationship with the therapist that involves meeting outside of the office. What should the CSW do to manage her ethical responsibilities in this case?

    a. Consider whether the earlier appointment was confidential.
    b. Inform the client that the existing relationship is not unethical as it has no negative impact on client care. Consider whether a similar relationship is possible with the current client.
    c. Scold the client for inquiring about the therapist's relationships.
    d. Cancel the coffee plan by phone with the client in the room, to acknowledge and take responsibility for her mistake.

7. A licensed CSW seeks to expand her private practice by hiring Associate CSWs. During the interview process with potential associates, the licensed CSW informs them that during each pay period, she organizes their clients by fee, from lowest to highest. The fees from the three lowest-paying sessions will be fully retained by the licensee. For all remaining sessions, the Associate will be paid $20/hour, regardless of how much the client actually paid. The licensed CSW tells interviewees that this structure is designed to keep her from losing money on sessions where the client does not pay, or where the associate chooses to work pro bono. The appropriate response from interviewees would be to:

   a. Inform the supervisor that this fee arrangement is not legal and advise her to make changes in her contracting
   b. Inform the supervisor that this fee arrangement is potentially problematic, and inquire as to whether alternate arrangements are possible
   c. Seek to obtain the job, and then once hired into the fee arrangement, file a formal wage complaint with the state
   d. Suggest an alternate contract where supervisees are prohibited from working pro bono, and clients are charged automatically based on a credit card on file

8. A 13-year-old girl presents for treatment at a nonprofit agency that provides no-cost therapy. The girl is assigned to an CSW. The CSW determines the girl is not in crisis. The girl says she is suffering from distress related to family conflict. Legally, the appropriate first step for the CSW at this point is to:

   a. Contact the girl's parents to seek consent for treatment
   b. Assess the girl's emotional maturity
   c. Proceed with therapy, and involve the girl's parents
   d. Assess whether the girl is engaging in substance abuse

9. A client diagnosed with a moderate Anxiety Disorder calls her therapist, who is an CSW, at the client's scheduled session time. The client informs the therapist that the client will be unable to attend today's scheduled session and asks the CSW whether they could do a phone session instead. Which step is a necessary part of the CSW addressing their legal responsibilities?

   a. Inform the client that the CSW must have certification in telehealth to engage in phone sessions.
   b. Go forward with the session as scheduled, and assess for potential crisis.
   c. Determine and document the client's specific location.
   d. Inform the client that while a phone session is not allowed, they can have a session through telehealth if the client can meet using a HIPAA-compliant videoconference platform.

10. An CSW is working with an 80-year-old client who has been diagnosed with a depressive disorder. The client tells the CSW she is ready to die, and has a plan to die by suicide the next day. The client explains that she had led a full life, and wants to control how she dies "before age takes that control away from me." How should the CSW fulfill their legal responsibilities in this case?

    a. Seek immediate consultation.
    b. Contact the local adult protective service agency.
    c. Intervene as needed to prevent the threatened suicide.
    d. Assess whether the client is otherwise of sound mind, and if so, honor their choice.

Batting practice: Answers and rationales

As always, it's useful to carefully review not only what answers are correct and incorrect, but also *why* the various answers are right and wrong.

Batting Practice

1. Your client is suing her employer, saying that long hours and stressful working conditions caused her anxiety disorder. You receive a subpoena from the employer's attorney, calling on you to produce the client's records and to testify in the case. You contact your client, who asks you not to testify or share her records. You should:

   a. **Incorrect.** Advise her to drop or settle her lawsuit, since you will likely be required to testify and to share her records.
   b. **CORRECT.** Respond to the subpoena by asserting privilege.
   c. **Incorrect.** Waive privilege on the client's behalf, since an exception to privilege applies.
   d. **Incorrect.** Provide no response to the subpoena, since it did not come from a judge.

The correct answer is B. While an exception to privilege does apply here, only the client or a judge can waive privilege. Until you know that either the client has waived privilege or a judge has determined that privilege does not apply, asserting privilege is a good default position. You also can get there by process of elimination: A is an incorrect response because giving the client legal advice would be outside of a CSW's scope of practice; C would be an incorrect response since it is never up to the therapist to determine whether privilege will be waived; and D is an incorrect response because failure to respond to a subpoena is not advisable.

2. A client who recently moved out of state leaves her former therapist, a California CSW, a voicemail to ask that the CSW forward her file to the client's new therapist where she now lives. Considering the CSW's legal responsibilities, the CSW should:

    a. **Incorrect.** Release the file directly to the client.
    b. **CORRECT.** Contact the client and ask the client to submit a signed release authorizing the file to be sent.
    c. **Incorrect.** Contact the licensing board of the client's new home state to determine applicable laws there for disclosure of health information.
    d. **Incorrect.** Contact the client's new therapist and ask the therapist and the client to sign a release authorizing the file to be sent.

It is legal to release a client's file to a third party with the client's permission. Therapists are not limited to only releasing records to the client themselves (A). When the intended recipient is a third party, it is the client authorizing the release (B); the third party does not need to sign the request (D). Because the original CSW is based in California, it is California's disclosure laws that would apply, not those in the client's new home state (C).

3. You are working with a Latina mother and her 7-year-old son in therapy, when you observe unusual bruises on the boy's face and arms. The bruises seem to be in several different stages of healing. When you ask how he got the bruises, both the boy and his mother refuse to answer. You should:

    a. **CORRECT.** Report suspected child abuse.
    b. **Incorrect.** Consider whether physical discipline is common in Latin cultures.
    c. **Incorrect.** Remind the mother of the limits of confidentiality.
    d. **Incorrect.** Ask the child to remove his shirt to inspect his torso for additional injuries.

While the injuries, and both clients' response to the therapist's inquiries, are not a guarantee that abuse has taken place, remember that the therapist does not need to be certain. They just need to reasonably suspect abuse. The location of the injuries, the fact that they are in multiple stages of healing, and the refusal to explain them would amount to reasonable suspicion in almost any CSW's mind. B would not be correct because the abuse reporting standards do not change on the basis of client culture. C is not correct because it would be an insufficient response to what appears to be abuse. D is not correct because this would place the CSW in the role of an investigator, which is not the proper role of a therapist.

4. An Associate CSW has been working under supervision in a private practice setting for two years. The Associate achieves licensure, and informs the supervisor that the Associate will be starting their own private practice. The now-former Associate would like to bring their current clients along to the new practice. How can the Associate CSW best address their ethical responsibilities?

- a. **CORRECT.** Understand that the clients are ultimately clients of the supervisor, and allow the clients to determine how they wish to proceed.
- b. **Incorrect.** Understand that the clients are ultimately clients of the supervisor, and allow the supervisor to determine which clients may follow the new licensee into their private practice.
- c. **Incorrect.** Retain the files for all clients who wish to follow the new licensee into their private practice, allowing the supervisor to make copies if the supervisor wishes.
- d. **Incorrect.** Allow the clients to determine whether to follow the new licensee into private practice, paying the supervisor a fee for each client who does so. This fee covers the supervisor's costs for marketing that brought the clients in to see the Associate originally.

While supervisors bear ultimate responsibility for client well-being, clients retain their freedom of choice when it comes to selecting their treatment provider. The supervisor cannot make that choice for them (B). Files are the property of the employer, not the clinician seeing the client (C); clients following the new licensee to private practice would actually need to sign releases allowing the new licensee to copy current files and bring them along to the new practice. And paying a fee for referrals is explicitly prohibited by both ethical code and state law (D).

Batting Practice

5. Your client has health insurance, but the insurance carrier is refusing to cover the client's therapy because she is seeing you for couple therapy and does not, in your assessment, qualify for a diagnosis of mental illness. You should:

   a. **Incorrect.** Assess the client's ability to advocate on her own behalf with the insurance company.
   b. **Incorrect.** Offer to include an "insurance diagnosis" on the client's paperwork to facilitate coverage.
   c. **CORRECT.** Work with the client to develop an alternative plan for payment.
   d. **Incorrect.** Discontinue therapy.

It is legal and fairly common for insurers to provide coverage for therapy only in the presence of a diagnosed mental illness. As such, you will need to work with the client on an alternative plan for payment. A is incorrect because the client's ability to advocate is not relevant; the insurance carrier is within the rules to refuse coverage. B is incorrect as the creation of a diagnosis solely for the purposes of insurance coverage, when the therapist does not believe the client actually qualifies for the diagnosis, would likely be considered insurance fraud. D is incorrect because a sudden discontinuation of therapy could be considered abandonment. While termination due to unpaid fees is ethically acceptable, in this case the client may be able to simply pay out of pocket. Choosing to discontinue therapy would be premature.

Preparing for the 2019 California Clinical Social Work Law & Ethics Exam

6. The client of an CSW notices that before her session, as the CSW is escorting her previous appointment out of the office, the CSW and the person she is escorting out are discussing plans to have coffee together later. The client asks the CSW about this at the beginning of her session. The client tells the CSW that she, too, would like to have a more personal and social relationship with the therapist that involves meeting outside of the office. What should the CSW do to manage her ethical responsibilities in this case?

    a. **CORRECT.** Consider whether the earlier appointment was confidential.
    b. **Incorrect.** Inform the client that the existing relationship is not unethical as it has no negative impact on client care. Consider whether a similar relationship is possible with the current client.
    c. **Incorrect.** Scold the client for inquiring about the therapist's relationships.
    d. **Incorrect.** Cancel the coffee plan by phone with the client in the room, to acknowledge and take responsibility for her mistake.

We have to be careful about the assumptions we make. Therapists meet with a lot of people in our offices, not all of whom are clients. The person the CSW was escorting out of the office could have been a friend, a colleague, a business associate, or anything else. The CSW may want to be transparent with the client about the nature of that relationship, if they can legally and ethically do so. That transparency would reduce the client's concern that another client was receiving special treatment, and reinforce the boundaries of the therapist-client relationship.

7. A licensed CSW seeks to expand her private practice by hiring Associate CSWs. During the interview process with potential associates, the licensed CSW informs them that during each pay period, she organizes their clients by fee, from lowest to highest. The fees from the three lowest-paying sessions will be fully retained by the licensee. For all remaining sessions, the Associate will be paid $20/hour, regardless of how much the client actually paid. The licensed CSW tells interviewees that this structure is designed to keep her from losing money on sessions where the client does not pay, or where the associate chooses to work pro bono. The appropriate response from interviewees would be to:

    a. **Incorrect.** Inform the supervisor that this fee arrangement is not legal and advise her to make changes in her contracting

    b. **CORRECT.** Inform the supervisor that this fee arrangement is potentially problematic, and inquire as to whether alternate arrangements are possible

    c. **Incorrect.** Seek to obtain the job, and then once hired into the fee arrangement, file a formal wage complaint with the state

    d. **Incorrect.** Suggest an alternate contract where supervisees are prohibited from working pro bono, and clients are charged automatically based on a credit card on file

While the stated fee arrangement likely would represent a violation of law if any supervisee ever had only three sessions in a pay period (as they would make $0 for that pay period, obviously less than minimum wage), the supervisor hasn't failed to pay minimum wage *yet* -- they're just proposing a structure that could result in that. Despite the obvious concerns, the interviewees are likely not attorneys, and should not be providing legal advice to the employer (A). What they should do is seek out a pay structure that would always be in keeping with minimum wage law, and would not require the supervisees to violate their ethical standards. Since CSWs are encouraged to give a portion of their time to pro bono work, a contract prohibiting such work (D) would be troubling. Taking the job and filing a wage complaint without first at least discussing the issue with the employer (C) could be seen as a violation of ethical standards demanding respect and collaboration with colleagues.

Preparing for the 2019 California Clinical Social Work Law & Ethics Exam

8. A 13-year-old girl presents for treatment at a nonprofit agency that provides no-cost therapy. The girl is assigned to an CSW. The CSW determines the girl is not in crisis. The girl says she is suffering from distress related to family conflict. Legally, the appropriate first step for the CSW at this point is to:

   a. **Incorrect.** Contact the girl's parents to seek consent for treatment
   b. **CORRECT.** Assess the girl's emotional maturity
   c. **Incorrect.** Proceed with therapy, and involve the girl's parents
   d. **Incorrect.** Assess whether the girl is engaging in substance abuse

Minors as young as 12 can independently consent for mental health care so long as they are mature enough to participate intelligently in treatment. The CSW must make that determination to know whether consent for treatment can be present. Contacting the girl's parents to seek consent (A) would be necessary if the minor is assessed and determined not to be able to independently consent. Proceeding with therapy (C), and assessing for substance abuse (D), is appropriate after consent has been obtained.

Batting Practice

9. A client diagnosed with a moderate Anxiety Disorder calls her therapist, who is an CSW, at the client's scheduled session time. The client informs the therapist that the client will be unable to attend today's scheduled session and asks the CSW whether they could do a phone session instead. Which step is a necessary part of the CSW addressing their legal responsibilities?

    a. **Incorrect.** Inform the client that the CSW must have certification in telehealth to engage in phone sessions.
    b. **Incorrect.** Go forward with the session as scheduled, and assess for potential crisis.
    c. **CORRECT.** Determine and document the client's specific location.
    d. **Incorrect.** Inform the client that while a phone session is not allowed, they can have a session through telehealth if the client can meet using a HIPAA-compliant videoconference platform.

Phone sessions are legal (ruling out option D), and are considered telehealth. Telehealth has its own set of legal requirements that took effect July 1, 2016. Among those requirements is that the CSW must document the client's specific location (C) at every instance of telehealth. This serves in part to ensure that the therapist is not accidentally practicing across state lines. The CSW is not obligated to carry on with the session (B), and would be violating the law to go forward with the session without fulfilling their other telehealth responsibilities first. The CSW does not need specific telehealth certification (A) to engage in telehealth.

10. An LCSW is working with an 80-year-old client who has been diagnosed with a depressive disorder. The client tells the LCSW she is ready to die, and has a plan to die by suicide the next day. The client explains that she had led a full life, and wants to control how she dies "before age takes that control away from me." How should the LCSW fulfill their legal responsibilities in this case?

    a. **Incorrect.** Seek immediate consultation.
    b. **Incorrect.** Contact the local adult protective service agency.
    c. **CORRECT.** Intervene as needed to prevent the threatened suicide.
    d. **Incorrect.** Assess whether the client is otherwise of sound mind, and if so, honor their choice.

While California does now allow physician assisted suicide for terminally ill patients, that is not the situation here. This client expresses a suicide plan, and the LCSW has a legal responsibility to intervene consistent with the standards of the profession. Consultation (A) does not address the LCSW's responsibility. There is no abuse to report (B). The LCSW cannot legally honor the client's choice (D), even if the LCSW believes the client's choice is morally acceptable.

How did you do? If you struggled a bit with these, don't worry. They're a bit complex by design, and may be much more complex than the actual items on the test. If you are interested in taking a full-length practice test, well, that's up next.

You've got this.

Good luck!

Practice Test Information

Preparing for the 2019 California Clinical Social Work Law & Ethics Exam

Instructions

There are two answer sheets on the next two pages, which you can tear out of the book and fill in as you are taking the practice test. (There are *two* sheets there to give you two attempts at the test. Hopefully if you take the practice test a second time, your score increases.)

Use the practice test here as you see fit! There are a number of different ways you could use it to help you prepare:

1. **Focus on understanding.** In this study method, you would take a practice test untimed, focusing on carefully examining the question and thinking through the available responses. You would then spend a fair amount of time with the *rationale* for each correct answer, making sure that you are deeply understanding the underlying concepts. While of course you hope to get a good score, your scores on the practice exams are not terribly important when understanding is your goal. Any question you answer incorrectly is simply a chance to expand your knowledge and better prepare you for the real test. After all, while the actual test will cover the same content areas as these practice exams, it is unlikely they will ask the same questions in the same ways. You need to be able to understand and apply the key legal and ethical concepts across different clinical situations.

2. **Focus on timing.** In this study method, you would time yourself on each test, making sure you finish within the 90-minute time limit. This also gives you an opportunity to practice any anxiety management techniques you may need, and to practice time management skills like skipping questions you may want to come back to later. Many examinees have reported that they spent more time on the actual test than they did on practice tests, so it's good if you have at least some amount of time left over when you complete each of the tests here.

3. **Focus on performance.** In this study method, a good score is the only goal. As is the case in method 1 above, you still want to make sure you understand why you answered incorrectly on any items you got wrong, but this method is more about confidence-building leading up to your test day. One thing to note if you're focused on your score: Because practice tests (and the real thing, in different exam cycles) vary in difficulty, it is not safe to presume that a score on any given practice tests equates with roughly the same score on the real thing. If you're getting a significant majority of the items on a practice test right, your scores have been steadily improving, and you can understand why any incorrect answers you gave were incorrect, that is probably a better measure of preparedness than any specific score.

There are other, more creative ways you can use the material here as well, such as:

- Quizzing others in a study group
- Dividing the questions into three "mini-exams" of 25 questions each
- Going through questions and rationales one at a time, flash-card style

I'm a big believer in being pragmatic where studying for an exam is concerned. Do what you know works best for you.

A few cautionary notes

While these questions and responses are written to help prepare you for the California CSW Law and Ethics Exam, it is important to bear in mind that the practice tests here (like all practice tests) are *approximations* of the style and format of the exam itself. The actual exam changes with each 90-day test cycle; some exam cycles have a more difficult exam, while others have an easier exam. This is why the passing score changes with each cycle, to ensure that examinees aren't disadvantaged by happening into a tougher cycle of the test.

Preparing for the 2019 California Clinical Social Work Law & Ethics Exam

It's also worth noting that, while every effort has been made here to tie these questions with specific and identifiable legal and ethical principles, ethical decision-making isn't always clear-cut. Even on questions where these is a clear correct answer, reasonable arguments can sometimes be made for some of the other response choices. If you find yourself arguing with the rationale on a question, focus your efforts on understanding why the correct response was identified as such.

If you are using multiple practice tests from different sources (for example, if you are using this book alongside practice tests provided by a test prep company), you may find that in some instances, the different sources suggest different answers for similar questions. That can be confusing and anxiety-provoking, but usually has a good explanation. You may be able to find that even minor, technical differences between the questions account for the differences in the best answers. You may also find that one source or another has something wrong – either because the law or ethical standard has changed, or because it has been misinterpreted. All of us (myself included) make mistakes on occasion. Rest assured that for the actual exam, every item must be keyed to an objective standard, so there will always be a current, justifiable best answer. If you find yourself disagreeing with a practice item from any source, and you have a clear legal or ethical rationale supporting your response choice, you're probably in good shape for the actual test. And of course, if you'd like to discuss anything in this book that you think I may have incorrect, please email me at support@bencaldwelllabs.com and let me know.

Finally, you may find that some questions here resemble situations that you have actually encountered in your practice. Hopefully it would go without saying, but nothing here should be construed as legal advice or as a substitution for consulting with a qualified attorney. The kinds of case vignettes that are written for an exam are (by design) reductionist, focusing on only a few features of a case. Real-life decision-making is often more complex.

Answer Sheets

California CSW Law & Ethics

1. ____	21. ____	41. ____	61. ____
2. ____	22. ____	42. ____	62. ____
3. ____	23. ____	43. ____	63. ____
4. ____	24. ____	44. ____	64. ____
5. ____	25. ____	45. ____	65. ____
6. ____	26. ____	46. ____	66. ____
7. ____	27. ____	47. ____	67. ____
8. ____	28. ____	48. ____	68. ____
9. ____	29. ____	49. ____	69. ____
10. ____	30. ____	50. ____	70. ____
11. ____	31. ____	51. ____	71. ____
12. ____	32. ____	52. ____	72. ____
13. ____	33. ____	53. ____	73. ____
14. ____	34. ____	54. ____	74. ____
15. ____	35. ____	55. ____	75. ____
16. ____	36. ____	56. ____	
17. ____	37. ____	57. ____	
18. ____	38. ____	58. ____	
19. ____	39. ____	59. ____	
20. ____	40. ____	60. ____	

California CSW Law & Ethics

1. ___	21. ___	41. ___	61. ___
2. ___	22. ___	42. ___	62. ___
3. ___	23. ___	43. ___	63. ___
4. ___	24. ___	44. ___	64. ___
5. ___	25. ___	45. ___	65. ___
6. ___	26. ___	46. ___	66. ___
7. ___	27. ___	47. ___	67. ___
8. ___	28. ___	48. ___	68. ___
9. ___	29. ___	49. ___	69. ___
10. ___	30. ___	50. ___	70. ___
11. ___	31. ___	51. ___	71. ___
12. ___	32. ___	52. ___	72. ___
13. ___	33. ___	53. ___	73. ___
14. ___	34. ___	54. ___	74. ___
15. ___	35. ___	55. ___	75. ___
16. ___	36. ___	56. ___	
17. ___	37. ___	57. ___	
18. ___	38. ___	58. ___	
19. ___	39. ___	59. ___	
20. ___	40. ___	60. ___	

Practice Test

1. A CSW has a new client who explains during the intake session that she had a hard time coming into therapy. The client says that her previous therapist asked her to go on a date with him at their termination session. She refused, and has not spoken with the former therapist again, but the experience left her skeptical of therapists generally. Legally, the CSW must:

   a. Report the other therapist's actions to the BBS.
   b. Confront the other therapist on their behavior.
   c. Provide the client a copy of the brochure "Professional Therapy Never Includes Sex."
   d. Maintain the client's confidentiality.

2. An adult client who has been seeing a CSW in therapy for six months asks the CSW for a copy of her treatment record. Because the CSW has documented that she suspects the client is being dishonest in her denials of recent drug use, the CSW worries that sharing the file would harm the therapeutic relationship. The most appropriate course of action for the CSW would be to:

   a. Turn over the records as required by law, and use it as an opportunity to address the client's possible substance use.
   b. Provide the client with a partial copy of the file, leaving out the suspicion of recent drug use.
   c. Refuse to turn over the records, offer a treatment summary instead, and inform the client that if she wishes, she can select a neutral therapist to review the file.
   d. Submit the client's request, and the CSW's reason for refusing, to a district judge for review.

Practice Test

3. A group therapy client informs other group members that she has opened a bakery, and is willing to provide the other group members with a discount on purchases there. The client extends this offer to the CSW who facilitates the group, and clarifies that this is simply a way of saying "thank you" for running the group; the client does not expect any special treatment in return. The CSW must:

   a. Politely refuse the offer.
   b. Consider the clinical and cultural implications of accepting or rejecting the offer.
   c. Determine whether the value of the discount would be more than $25.
   d. Discourage group members from using the discount they have been offered.

4. A CSW receives a subpoena from the attorney for an Italian restaurant where a client of the CSW formerly worked. The subpoena requests the client's complete clinical record, and notes that the client is suing the restaurant over the client's firing. The client claims that the firing was discriminatory and caused damage to her mental health. How should the CSW respond to the subpoena?

   a. Contact the client, determine her wishes, and encourage her to allow the records to be released now since the situation is an exception to confidentiality.
   b. Contact the client, determine her wishes, and assert privilege if she desires.
   c. Contact the court, assert privilege, and do not respond directly to the restaurant's attorney since a private subpoena is not a court order.
   d. Contact the court, assert privilege, and respond to the subpoena by saying that records cannot be released without the client's signed consent.

5. A CSW is seeing a family for an intake session. The family includes three foster girls, ages 16, 13, and 10. During individual interviews with each of the children, they all reveal that they are currently in sexual relationships. The 16-year-old received treatment for a sexually transmitted disease a year ago after catching it from her then-17-year-old boyfriend. The 13-year-old says that she is having sex with her 14-year-old boyfriend. And the 10-year-old tells you that she is pregnant, though she will not reveal anything about the age or identity of the father. Which of these relationships must be reported as child abuse?

   a. All three children's relationships are reportable.
   b. The 16-year-old's relationship and the 10-year-old's relationship are reportable.
   c. Only the 13-year-old's relationship is reportable.
   d. Only the 10-year-old's relationship is reportable.

6. The 59-year-old client of a CSW calls her therapist from the hospital for a planned check-in conversation. The client tells the therapist she has been hospitalized for a severe respiratory infection and is likely to remain as an inpatient in the hospital for at least another two weeks. She also expresses a belief that hospital staff are stealing her belongings. The CSW should:

   a. Maintain the client's confidentiality.
   b. Report the client's belief to hospital staff.
   c. Report the client's accusation as suspected dependent adult abuse.
   d. Presume the client's accusation is a side effect of the pain

7. A client reports to her therapist, a CSW, that the client's antidepressant medication does not appear to be having a positive effect even after eight weeks of her taking the prescribed dosage. The CSW should:

  a. Encourage the client to request a medication change.
  b. Encourage the client to request a higher dosage to achieve the intended effect.
  c. Encourage the client to consult with her physician.
  d. Encourage the client to consider discontinuing the medication and focusing on efforts to improve her depressive symptoms through therapy.

8. A CSW is involved on a treatment team for a county social service agency. The CSW grows frustrated that the CSW's suggestions are rarely implemented by the team. An appropriate course of action would be for the CSW to:

  a. Seek advice from colleagues about handling treatment team dynamics.
  b. Temporarily stop providing input into team decisions until the CSW can better understand why previous suggestions have not been implemented.
  c. In the interest of transparency, directly inform clients of the CSW's recommendations, including those that the team has rejected.
  d. Demand that the team implement the CSW's suggestions to promote the well-being of clients.

9. A CSW is being interviewed for a podcast. The interviewers ask about her training and clinical work, and repeatedly refer to her as "Doctor," even though her highest degree is a master's degree. The CSW should:

   a. End the interview and ask that it not be released.
   b. No action is called for, as the interview does not qualify as advertising.
   c. Continue the interview, and afterward, remind the interviewer of her proper title.
   d. Politely correct the interviewers, and ensure that the correction is included on any edited version of the interview used in the podcast.

10. A family from Cambodia is seeing a CSW for family therapy. During a family session, the father tells the therapist that he sometimes disciplines his 15-year-old son the same way the father had been disciplined in Cambodia when he was young: With lashes across his back, using a stick. The mother voices her objection to this form of discipline, and notes that on multiple occasions the son was left bleeding and crying. The most appropriate action for the CSW would be to:

   a. Consider the cultural elements involved and inform the clients that such discipline may not be accepted in the US.
   b. Report suspected physical abuse to the local child protective service agency.
   c. Remind the family of the limits of confidentiality and ask whether there are any photos of the son's injuries.
   d. Consider the cultural elements involved and research common Cambodian disciplinary practices to determine whether the behavior is consistent with cultural norms.

Practice Test

11. A CSW shopping for clothing approaches the checkout counter and observes that the only worker at the cash register is a client of hers. The CSW should:

    a. Make her purchases as she normally would, behaving like an ordinary customer unless the client chooses to behave in a more familiar manner.
    b. Ask to speak with the store's manager, and explain that she needs to be checked out by a different worker, without providing any information on the reason why.
    c. Leave the store.
    d. Inform the client that, in order to protect the client's privacy, she will return to the store on a different day.

12. A 70-year-old client tells a CSW that the client had been under-medicated for several months while living at a nursing home in Florida the prior year. The CSW asks how the client knows this, and the client says that her prescription specifically noted that her medication should be given twice a day, but she received it only once each day. The CSW believes the client has good cognitive functioning. The CSW should:

    a. Report suspected elder abuse to the CSW's local adult protective service agency.
    b. Report suspected elder abuse to the adult protective service agency local to the nursing home in Florida.
    c. Encourage the client to report what happened to the appropriate adult protective service agency in Florida.
    d. Encourage the client to document the events for a possible civil lawsuit against the nursing home in Florida.

13. A 14-year-old girl presents for therapy at a local mental health clinic, where a CSW is assigned to her case. During a screening interview, the girl tells the CSW that she is struggling with anxiety around her schoolwork and social relationships. She goes on to say that she plans to pay for therapy on her own and would prefer that her parents not know she is in therapy. The CSW should:

   a. Assess the girl's ability to participate intelligently in therapy and determine whether notifying the parents would be damaging.
   b. Determine whether notifying the parents would be damaging and determine what adult can consent for the girl's therapy.
   c. Assess the girl's ability to participate intelligently in treatment and inform her that even when seen under her own consent, her parents may have the right to access her records if they become aware she is in therapy.
   d. Determine whether notifying the parents would be damaging and determine whether notifying the girl's school would be damaging.

14. A CSW provided therapy to a 16-year-old boy for several months with his parents' consent. A few months later, the CSW receives a subpoena from the attorney for a classmate of the boy. The classmate accused the client of physical assault, and the classmate's family is suing to recover medical expenses. The subpoena requests complete records of the boy's treatment. The CSW attempts to contact the client and his parents but is unsuccessful. The CSW should:

   a. Wait to respond to the subpoena until the CSW is able to determine how the client would like the CSW to respond.
   b. Wait to respond to the subpoena until the CSW is able to determine how the parents would like the CSW to respond.
   c. Respond to the subpoena by asserting privilege, and continue attempts to contact the client and his parents.
   d. Acknowledge the exception to privilege, turn over the client's records, and inform the client and his family as soon as possible.

Practice Test

15. A former client calls the CSW who had treated her two years earlier. The former client verbally requests that the CSW forward her file to her new therapist in a different state. The former client confirms her identity using her social security number and is able to identify specific topics of the prior therapy, leaving the CSW confident in the identity of the caller. The CSW should:

   a. Take down the information for the new therapist and forward the file as the client requested.
   b. Take down the information for the new therapist, contact that therapist, and have that therapist complete a written records request.
   c. Take down the information for the new therapist, and inform the former client that she will need to request that the records be released directly to her. She can then forward the file to the new therapist if she so chooses.
   d. Take down the information for the new therapist, and send the former client appropriate paperwork to request in writing that her file be released.

16. A potential client with partial paralysis contacts a CSW and asks whether he may receive therapy by phone for his symptoms of depression. The CSW assesses the potential client by phone and determines he is appropriate for phone-based services. Legally, the CSW must:

   a. Obtain consent for phone-based services and inform the potential client of the possible risks and benefits.
   b. Obtain consent in writing for phone-based services and inform the potential client that such services are currently considered experimental in nature.
   c. Assess the client in person at least once before moving to phone-based services.
   d. Assess the client in person and identify the closest hospital emergency room to the client, in case of emergency.

17. A social worker has been working with a family for several sessions and plans a session where the entire family will participate in a ceremony relieving the oldest daughter of the responsibility she has taken on as a co-parent. Shortly before the session, the mother informs the CSW that she will be away on a business trip and asks whether she can participate in the session by phone or videoconferencing. The mother's frequent absences are part of the reason why the daughter felt obligated to take on parenting tasks. The social worker should:

  a. Contact the BBS to see whether the CSW can include the mother in session while she is on her trip.
  b. Include the mother in the session and in the ceremony via phone or videoconference, and clarify that her involvement is consultation rather than therapy.
  c. Refuse the mother's request and reschedule the ceremony for a time she can attend in person.
  d. Contact the other family members to see whether they believe including the mother would be legally and ethically appropriate.

18. A walk-in client at a local counseling center presents with moderate suicidal ideation and racing thoughts. The front desk worker at the clinic tells an available CSW that the client should be seen immediately, and that the clinic manager has approved skipping the usual intake paperwork to get the client in to see the CSW as quickly as possible, as the client has verbally agreed to be seen. Legally, the CSW should:

  a. Inform the client of the fee for services, and the basis on which the fee is computed, prior to beginning treatment.
  b. Demand that the client complete the full standard intake paperwork for the clinic prior to beginning treatment.
  c. Inform the client of the limits of confidentiality prior to beginning treatment.
  d. Demand that the clinic manager provide approval in writing for skipping the usual intake paperwork, in order to reduce the CSW's potential liability.

Practice Test

19. A CSW working primarily with Jewish clients learns from one such client that the client, as well as two other clients of the CSW, attend the same synagogue. The three had discussed their therapist over lunch one day, describing traits that they did and did not like about the CSW's work. The CSW should:

   a. Consider whether the clients' discussion of each other in therapy would impair clinical judgment or increase the risk of exploitation.
   b. Remind all three clients of the limits of confidentiality.
   c. Encourage all three clients to share as little from their therapeutic work as possible, to preserve their independent therapeutic relationships with the CSW.
   d. Ask that the clients not discuss anything about each other or their shared synagogue in session, focusing instead on the issues and relationships unique to each client.

20. An associate CSW has been struggling with a difficult family case. The associate's supervisor suggests that the associate record video of future sessions so that the associate and supervisor can together review what happens in session. The associate is reluctant to record sessions, fearing that the parents in the family might feel embarrassed. The associate CSW is required to:

   a. Remind the clients that, because the associate is under supervision, video recording of sessions is a common and accepted practice.
   b. Obtain specific consent for recording from each adult family member prior to recording sessions.
   c. Comply with the supervisor's request even if the family would prefer to not be recorded, as the associate is working under the supervisor's license.
   d. Remind the clients of the limits of confidentiality prior to recording sessions.

21. A 20-year-old woman seeks the services of a CSW. The woman explains to the therapist that she would like individual therapy to help her get along better with her college roommate. Ethically, the CSW should:

   a. Refer the client to at least three local therapists qualified to treat the problem, as it is outside the CSW's scope of practice.
   b. Refer the client to at least three local therapists qualified to treat the problem, as it is outside the CSW's scope of competence.
   c. Inform the client of the potential risks and benefits of treatment.
   d. Inform the client that she will need to bring the roommate into therapy with her.

22. Two clients in a therapy group have become friends outside of the group. They often arrive to group together and appear to share inside jokes during the group. Other group members express concern to the CSW running the group that they are being made fun of or that what they share in the group may come up between these two friends outside of group. The CSW should:

   a. Encourage concerned members to express their concerns in the group.
   b. Reassure concerned members that ethically the two friends cannot share information from the group outside of the group context.
   c. Remove one of the two friends from the group and refer them to another group.
   d. Demand that the two members who have become friends explain to the group the nature of their friendship and any group-related conversations they have had outside of the group.

Practice Test

23. An individual client acknowledges to her therapist (a CSW) that she lied on the CSW's intake form and actually does have several past suicide attempts in her history. She says she is not feeling suicidal now, though she has recently experienced the ending of a romantic relationship and the death of a distant relative. Legally, the CSW should:

a. Complete a No Harm Contract with the client.
b. Discontinue therapy and refer the client to a higher level of care, as she is high risk.
c. Initiate the process of involuntary hospitalization.
d. Assess further and break confidentiality if required to resolve any threat of suicide.

24. A CSW is working with an individual client who was recently fired in a way the client experienced as humiliating. The client tells the therapist that he intends to go this weekend to the office building where he had worked, ensure no people are present in the building, and as long as no people would be endangered, burn the building down. "I know their insurance would cover the losses," the client says, "I just want to make a point." Legally, the CSW must:

a. Report the threat to the business to ensure that all current employees are protected.
b. Report the threat to local police, providing minimal additional information about how the CSW knows of the threat.
c. Warn the client that unless he takes back his threat, the CSW must break confidentiality to protect the employees of the business.
d. No specific action is required.

Preparing for the 2019 California Clinical Social Work Law & Ethics Exam

25. A CSW in private practice is concluding her last session of the day. After the session ends, the client pays her fee by credit card and schedules their next meeting, and both CSW and client walk out of the building where the practice is located. There, the CSW realizes she has had forgotten her wallet and does not have the cash to cover her usual bus fare to get home. The client offers cash to pay the therapist's bus fare. When the CSW initially refuses the offer, the client suggests that the money simply be credited toward the next session's fee. Ethically, the therapist should:

   a. Politely refuse the offer and find another way to get home.
   b. Accept the offer under the condition that it is a prepayment of part of the next session fee.
   c. Offer to immediately provide a partial session for which the client could pay a small amount of cash for professional services.
   d. Accept the offer, keep the transaction separate from payments for therapy, and repay the client in cash at the beginning of the next session.

26. A CSW covered by HIPAA plans to move her office approximately five miles and has hired a moving company to transport all of her office furniture, supplies, and equipment. How should the therapist address the file cabinets that contain hard copy client files?

   a. Hire an additional security contractor approved by HIPAA to oversee the move and ensure records are transported without security breaches.
   b. Ask the moving company to provide a Business Associate Agreement establishing that they will abide by the rules HIPAA sets forth regarding privacy and security of client data.
   c. Remove all files and transport them herself, as HIPAA requires that contractors not be given access to client records without client consent.
   d. Demand that every employee of the moving company that will be working on her move sign a privacy statement agreeing to follow strict security standards.

Practice Test

27. A client who has expressed great concern about anyone knowing she is in therapy passes out in the middle of a session. The CSW the client was seeing is able to wake her long enough to learn that she has recently been struggling with illness and has pain from a neck injury, and the CSW knows from the client's intake paperwork that she has a blood disorder. The CSW should:

   a. Stay with the client and continue attempting to wake her.
   b. Call 911 and transport the client outside of the office into a public area to protect her privacy.
   c. Call 911 and summon paramedics without providing any information about the client or her illness.
   d. Call 911, summon paramedics, and inform them of the client's medical issues.

28. A CSW who is new to the community seeks to build her referral base so that she can grow her practice. For those colleagues who refer clients to her, she calls the colleague (without revealing any information about the client) and offers to buy the colleague lunch to say thanks and engage in professional networking. An established CSW in the community receives such an offer from the new CSW after referring a client to the new CSW. How should the established CSW respond?

   a. Accept the invitation under the condition that they each agree to pay their own bill.
   b. Decline the invitation and report the new CSW to the BBS.
   c. Accept the invitation under the condition that no client information will be discussed.
   d. Accept the invitation and request a release of information from the client allowing the established CSW to discuss the case with the new CSW.

29. A CSW is surprised to see that her new client did not complete the CSW's standard informed consent paperwork in the waiting room prior to their scheduled session. The CSW brings the client into her therapy office, where the client says that he can only read and write in Spanish. He speaks English fluently, and says he prefers that his therapy sessions be in English. The CSW only speaks and writes in English. Ethically, the therapist should:

   a. Have a verbal conversation to establish informed consent, and have the client sign the informed consent document.
   b. Have a verbal conversation to establish informed consent, and document that conversation in session notes.
   c. Provide a Spanish language translation of her informed consent documents as soon as possible, for the client to read and sign.
   d. Have a verbal conversation about informed consent, and offer to provide a Spanish language translation of her informed consent documents as soon as possible.

30. A CSW learns that his individual client, who is being seen for symptoms of Bipolar Disorder, is also interested in attending couple therapy with her spouse. The client asks the CSW whether the couple could see the CSW together for couple therapy separately from her individual sessions, and says she is willing to sign a release form such that information from her individual sessions could be discussed in couple therapy and vice versa. Ethically, the CSW should:

   a. Continue individual treatment with the client and refer out for the couple therapy.
   b. Continue individual treatment with the client and begin concurrent couple therapy, utilizing a separate file with a separate treatment plan.
   c. Conduct a screening interview with the couple, as well as with each partner individually, to assess whether adding couple therapy to the client's existing treatment plan would be appropriate.
   d. Discontinue the individual treatment in order to begin couple treatment, with the client's release in place to allow for material from the individual sessions to be discussed in couple work.

Practice Test

31. A CSW is working with a family where the parents are in the process of getting a divorce and are arguing over custody of their two children. Therapy has focused on maintaining effective co-parenting, as neither parent wants an extended court battle. Because the CSW knows the family well and has seen both parents interacting with the children, the parents ask the CSW to submit a letter to the court with the CSW's clinical evaluation of each of their parenting skills. The best course of action for the CSW would be to:

    a. Obtain a release from all family members, and send the letter to the court, emphasizing that the evaluative statements should not be used to draw conclusions about custody.
    b. Obtain a release from all family members, and send the letter to the court, offering specific recommendations for custody based on the CSW's work with the family and based on the CSW's knowledge of the wishes of the children.
    c. Obtain a release from all family members, and engage in a process of testing and evaluation to draw objective conclusions before completing the letter.
    d. Refuse to send the letter.

32. An adult client tells a CSW that the client's 89-year-old mother is in hospice care. The client goes on to say that the hospice staff have been screening the mother's mail and phone calls, as they are concerned that she would fall prey to financial scammers who target the elderly. The client tells the CSW that the mother has severe dementia and that the client believes the screening of mail and phone calls is appropriate. The client also says the staff has never refused him access to his mother. The CSW should:

    a. Obtain a release from the client, contact the hospice directly, and gather more information about the mother's diagnosis and the need for mail and calls to be screened.
    b. Report suspected elder abuse.
    c. Maintain the client's confidentiality.
    d. Empower the client to gather more information on the mother's diagnosis and the need for mail and calls to be screened, and ask the client to bring that information to a future session for the client and the CSW to review together.

33. A CSW learns that her client's adopted son was recently involved in a series of hit-and-run accidents. At present, law enforcement is investigating but does not know who is responsible. The client expresses fear of all possible outcomes; if the police determine it was her son, the son will likely go to jail. If the police do not determine it was her son, the son may continue with his risky and damaging behavior. The client says she does not want to turn her son in. Considering her legal and ethical obligations, the CSW should:

   a. Report the son to law enforcement as a potential danger to others.
   b. Anonymously report the son's actions to law enforcement, without revealing the name of the therapist or the client, and without revealing how the CSW came to know the information.
   c. Encourage the client to report the son to law enforcement to reduce the risk that he will harm others in the future.
   d. Discuss the client's feelings in greater detail and examine the risks and benefits of various possible courses of action while maintaining the client's confidentiality.

34. A CSW is distressed to learn that a former client has posted a detailed account of the client's therapy online in the form of an article. While the article is mostly positive, it mentions the CSW by name and includes some incorrect information about the CSW's qualifications. The CSW notices that it is possible to leave comments on the article. The CSW should:

   a. Post a comment in response to the article, thanking the author while also correcting the errors.
   b. Contact the site owners to ask that the article be taken down, without specifying whether the writer was actually a client.
   c. Contact the former client directly to encourage them to correct the article.
   d. No action is called for.

Practice Test

35. A CSW is working with an individual client who is employed in the movie industry. The client is emotionally unstable following a breakup. The client informs the CSW that the client will be travelling out of state for the next three weeks to work on a film, and asks whether the CSW can continue to work with the client by phone during that time. The CSW should first:

   a. Assess the severity of the client's symptoms to determine whether phone therapy is appropriate, and if so, proceed with phone sessions.
   b. Determine whether they have the requisite qualifications to practice in the state to which the client is travelling.
   c. Determine the client's state of residency.
   d. Inquire with the BBS as to the appropriateness and legality of phone sessions for this client.

36. A polyamorous couple experiencing difficulty in their sexual relationship presents for therapy with a CSW who believes sexual activity outside of a monogamous relationship is inappropriate and harmful. The couple does not believe that their sexual relationships outside of their own relationship are causing their sexual problems with each other. Ethically, the CSW should:

   a. Seek to address underlying emotional issues that may be impacting the couple's sexual relationship, so as to improve the relationship without directly discussing the couple's other partners.
   b. Refer the couple to a therapist who does not share the CSW's belief.
   c. Inform the clients in advance of her belief, allowing the clients to determine whether they would like to continue therapy with her.
   d. Begin therapy by explaining her belief and the underlying research, and explaining that the couple's theory that their polyamory is not related to their own sexual difficulty is unlikely to be true.

37. A CSW's client confesses to her that he is struggling with guilt over his involvement in three recent gang-related murders. Two adults were killed: one was a rival gang member, the other was an innocent bystander. The third victim was also a rival gang member, and was just 17 years old. The client tells the CSW that he does not believe he or the others in his gang will be caught, but this is only worsening his guilt. How should the CSW handle her legal obligations surrounding confidentiality?

   a. Break confidentiality for the three murders and work with law enforcement to warn other members of the rival gang.
   b. Break confidentiality for the murder of the bystander and work with law enforcement to warn other members of the rival gang.
   c. Break confidentiality for the murder of the 17-year-old, and otherwise maintain confidentiality.
   d. Maintain the client's confidentiality for all past acts, and encourage him to consider self-reporting to law enforcement if necessary to resolve his guilt.

38. A CSW finds herself becoming increasingly blunt and even harsh with a client who is overweight and experiencing depression. The CSW realizes she is judging the client for the client's weight and her apparent lack of interest in resolving any of the personal or relational struggles that the CSW believes are perpetuating the client's depressive symptoms. The client continues attending therapy and reporting attempts to complete homework assigned by the therapist, but without improvement. The CSW should:

   a. Seek consultation and attempt to repair the therapeutic relationship.
   b. Seek consultation and refer the client to a therapist who does not share the CSW's weight bias.
   c. Refer the client out and seek additional training to recognize and not blame the client for common correlates to depression.
   d. Refer the client out as it does not appear that therapy has a reasonable likelihood of success.

Practice Test

39. A CSW is close to successful termination with a father who has been in treatment for 15 sessions. The father expresses his gratitude to the CSW, and says he would like to find a way to help families with similar needs. The CSW is aware of an online discussion group where the father could share his experience in therapy, steering potential clients toward the CSW and offering hope to families experiencing similar problems to the ones his own family had experienced at the beginning of therapy. Ethically, the CSW should:

   a. Encourage the father to share his experience in the discussion group, including both positive and negative components, and including the CSW's name so that other participants know where they can receive confidential help.
   b. Thank the father for his work in therapy, and discuss potential benefits and risks of several potential means by which the father could help similar families.
   c. Thank the father for his work in therapy, and discourage him from publicly sharing his experience in the interest of confidentiality.
   d. Encourage the father to share his experience in the discussion group but to do so anonymously, only naming the CSW if he chooses to do so.

40. A mother arrives late for her therapy session and is enraged. She reports that she just spent an hour dealing with police, who came to the grocery store where her car was parked and were about to break a window when she returned to the car and stopped them. The police, she said, rudely lectured her about the infant son she had left in the car while she was grocery shopping. While the car was in sunlight, it was only about 80 degrees out at the time and she had been away from the car for less than 20 minutes, she said. The CSW should:

   a. Explore the mother's feelings of anger and shame.
   b. Assess whether the son had suffered any harm.
   c. Ask for a Release of Information and offer to contact police directly to follow up.
   d. Report suspected child neglect.

41. A CSW is interested in conducting research on her clients, in an effort to determine whether a new form of treatment developed by the CSW is superior to existing treatments. Because the CSW already has access to the client files and would be reporting statistics on her treatment results, without specifics of any individual cases, she prepares to conduct an analysis of cases she has closed over the prior year. She hopes to publish the results of her research in a prominent journal. Ethically, the CSW should:

    a. Contact those former clients, inform them of the risks and benefits of involvement in the research, and determine their willingness to have their file included as one of those analyzed.
    b. Take steps to protect the confidentiality of individual cases, but include all cases from the prior year in her analysis to eliminate possible selection bias.
    c. Contact those former clients to let them know that their files have been included in her research.
    d. Because she is working with archival data that will be reported in aggregate, no action is required.

42. A client is aware of a local wellness center that is soon to be put up for sale. The client tells her therapist, a CSW, about the business and how much she would like to join the CSW in buying it. She presents a detailed proposal that would have them end their therapy relationship so that they could become investment partners. The CSW should:

    a. Carefully consider the risks and benefits associated with the potential investment.
    b. Remind the client of the boundaries of the therapy relationship.
    c. Inform the client that the CSW will only consider terminating therapy if it is clinically appropriate, and that any potential investment partnership could only be discussed once the therapeutic relationship has ended.
    d. Thank the client for her consideration in bringing the opportunity to the CSW, and suggest other possible investment partners.

43. A CSW has recently completed his hours of supervised experience and successfully completed the examination process, earning full licensure as a CSW. He is in the process of leaving the clinic where he worked as an associate, and setting up a private practice. In his last two weeks at the clinic, he tells his clients about his planned move. Many of his clients ask to see him at his new private practice once it opens rather than continuing treatment with a different therapist at the clinic. The CSW should:

a. Inform his supervisor of those clients' plans, make copies of their records, and take the originals to his new practice, leaving the copies with the agency.
b. Ensure that all fees for continuing clients will be the same at his private practice as they were at the clinic.
c. Ask each client who is planning to continue at his private practice to sign a Release of Information, authorizing the clinic to release the client's records to the CSW.
d. Politely refuse to see clients at his new practice, as these clients are clients of the clinic and must continue treatment there.

44. A CSW develops a friendly relationship with a physician who works in an adjacent building. The CSW asks the physician to refer any patients who need mental health services to the CSW, and provides a stack of $25 coupons the physician can give to patients to encourage them to contact the CSW. The CSW would apply that $25 toward the fee for the first session. The CSW should:

   a. Maintain the referral relationship, but discontinue the use of coupons.
   b. Discontinue the referral relationship, and market directly to prospective clients.
   c. Ensure that new clients referred from the physician are fully aware of all fees to be charged.
   d. Maintain the referral relationship, discontinue the use of coupons, ensure all clients pay the same fee for services, and thank the physician for referrals by directly paying the physician $25 for each new client she refers.

45. A Caucasian CSW receives a phone call from a prospective new client couple. The couple reports that they moved to the US from India three years ago, and they would like to come to therapy to work on communication difficulty in their marriage. The CSW strives to maintain strong awareness of cultural issues, but has never worked with anyone from India before. The best course of action for the CSW would be to:

   a. Refer the couple to a therapist of Indian descent.
   b. Encourage the clients to educate the CSW about Indian culture and customs.
   c. Seek resources and consultation to become familiar with Indian culture and customs, and to understand how Indian clients typically present in therapy.
   d. Wait until the clients come in for an initial assessment to determine whether meaningful cultural differences exist.

Practice Test

46. A famous actor contacts a CSW seeking help with his anxiety. Because he is so well-known, the actor expresses concern that the fact that he is in therapy could be "leaked" to the media, making it harder for him to be cast in desirable roles. He asks the CSW whether he can pay solely in cash so that the CSW will not have financial records, and he asks the CSW to keep records for treatment under a fake name that the actor would use when signing all treatment-related documents. How should the CSW respond?

   a. Refuse the requests.
   b. Refuse the request to keep records under a fake name, but allow the client to sign all documentation using whatever fake name they choose.
   c. Honor the request to keep treatment records under a fake name, but refuse the request to not keep financial records.
   d. Agree to both requests to protect the client's privacy while otherwise maintaining the terms of treatment.

47. A client mandated for treatment by his county probation office returns to therapy after a six-month absence. He informs the CSW that he needs records of his progress in treatment sent to his probation officer before his next court date, and provides a Release of Information allowing those records to be sent. However, he carries a balance due of more than $500 from sessions he attended but did not pay for prior to being absent from therapy. The CSW should:

   a. Continue with treatment at a reduced fee, and refuse to turn over records until at least a portion of the balance is paid.
   b. Continue with treatment at a reduced fee, and refuse to turn over records until the outstanding balance is paid in full.
   c. Consider terminating the client if he will be unable to pay his balance, and turn over records to the probation officer.
   d. Consider terminating the client if he will be unable to pay his balance, and notify the probation officer of the outstanding balance.

48. A CSW conducting her fourth home visit with a high-conflict family in poverty sees suitcases in their living room. When the CSW asks about the suitcases, the family's 15-year-old daughter announces that she is moving out, with plans to live with friends. She is not willing to provide the names of those friends or any other information to her family or to the CSW. The CSW should:

   a. Report the case to the CSW's local child protective service agency, as the 15-year-old is at high risk for abuse or neglect.
   b. Attempt to gain more information about the daughter's plans.
   c. Consider hospitalizing the daughter as a protective measure.
   d. Focus clinical attention on the parents, noting that they will be the ones around to continue clinical work, and terminate with the 15-year-old.

49. A CSW working in a middle school setting is confronted by a parent who is upset that the CSW has not filed a child abuse report over the bullying her daughter has faced. The daughter is regularly taunted by other girls at the school and has been injured in some shoving matches. Though the daughter has sought to avoid these fights and does not fight back, the CSW defends herself by noting that in each case the girl has been fighting with other girls around the same age and size. The daughter is a regular client of the CSW, and the mother has attended some sessions. The CSW should:

   a. Contact her local child protective service agency to report the mother for failing to protect her child.
   b. Contact her local child protective service agency to report physical abuse of the daughter.
   c. Contact the school principal to discuss the mother's concerns.
   d. Calmly explain to the mother why her daughter's injuries are not considered problematic.

Practice Test

50. The individual client of a CSW tells the CSW that he recently took his 94-year-old grandfather, who has been suffering from dementia, on a fishing trip to a nearby lake in a California State Park. He had grown frustrated with the quality of care the grandfather had been receiving at his nursing home, which he said was not adequate to the grandfather's medical needs. He also wanted to give his grandfather "one last hurrah," as he was concerned the grandfather's death was just weeks away. He was angry that the nursing home staff had berated him upon their return for not notifying them he was taking the grandfather for the weekend. The CSW should:

a. Report the nursing home for inadequate care, and the client for kidnapping.
b. Report the nursing home for inadequate care.
c. Report the client for kidnapping.
d. Ask the client to clarify how the nursing home's care is inadequate.

51. During an unusually tense family session, a mother confronts a CSW on the CSW's recent filing of a written report of suspected child abuse. The mother feels violated and reports that she can no longer trust the CSW. Other family members attempt to calm the mother, but share her concerns. The CSW should:

a. Discontinue treatment, as the therapeutic relationship has been irreparably compromised.
b. Remind the family of the limits of confidentiality, and seek to regain the family's trust.
c. In the interest of full disclosure, inform the mother that follow-up reports to the local child protective service agency may be necessary.
d. Ask to speak to the other family members without the mother present, to determine whether there is an appropriate path forward for therapy.

52. A CSW who has had a long and successful career working primarily with high-powered business executives and their families wants to write a tell-all book detailing the cases he saw in his practice and the lessons he learned from his clients, some of whom are well-known in the business and technology worlds. The best course of action for the CSW would be to:

a. Wait at least seven years since the last professional contact with all clients, at which point their records are no longer confidential.
b. Surrender his license and professional association membership prior to writing the book, so that no action can be taken against him for using client names.
c. Falsify any identifying information about each client he discusses.
d. Sell the book exclusively outside of California, to protect former clients from having friends and neighbors read about their clinical experiences.

53. A CSW worked with a woman in individual therapy for six months, focusing on treatment of depression symptoms following the client's messy divorce. The client improved significantly in therapy and terminated successfully. One year later, the CSW has been dating a man for two months when the CSW realizes the man is the ex-husband of the former client. The CSW should:

a. Discontinue the romantic relationship.
b. Contact the former client to determine her wishes. Given the amount of time that has passed and the success of treatment, she is likely to give her blessing.
c. Self-report to the BBS to seek their guidance on the most appropriate way to proceed.
d. No action is called for.

Practice Test

54. A CSW is studying a group therapy process for adolescents who have been victims of child abuse. The parents of one of the members of the group ask to have their 16-year-old child removed from the group and from the study, noting that they believe the group is making the child's trauma symptoms worse. The parents had been informed of this risk prior to agreeing to put their child in the study. The CSW should:

   a. Remind the parents of the agreement they signed outlining the risks of the research, and attempt to convince them to keep their child in the group.
   b. Remind the parents of the agreement they signed outlining the risks of the research, and leave the decision about participation up to the child.
   c. Remove the child from the group, and take steps to resolve any negative impacts the group caused for the child.
   d. Take steps to resolve any negative impacts the group caused for the child, and keep the child in the group based on the parents' initial agreement.

55. A CSW works across the street from a major software company's offices. The CSW begins advertising specifically to employees of the company, using the company's logo on the CSW's website and business cards to say that the CSW is "now proudly serving employees of" that company. One client, who works for the software company and had found the CSW through the website, asks about the relationship between the CSW and the software company. The CSW should:

   a. Clarify for the client that there is no formal relationship, and that the CSW simply enjoys working with employees of the company.
   b. Change the website and business cards to not use the company's logo.
   c. Seek to develop a more formal relationship with the company, including a contract to treat their employees.
   d. Change the website and business cards to indicate that the company's logo is a registered trademark used with permission.

56. A client comes to a CSW looking for treatment that her insurance will help pay for. The CSW has a waiting list for new clients. The CSW is the only CSW in the client's rural community, however, the CSW is aware of two counselors and one Psychologist in the community who may be able to treat the client immediately. The CSW should:

    a. Put the client on the CSW's waiting list.
    b. Inform the client of the other local providers.
    c. Contact the insurance company to determine whether they generally pay for the services of LCSWs or Psychologists.
    d. Base all referral decisions exclusively on the client's diagnosis.

57. Three CSWs working in different private practices in the same city share their frustrations with poor pay and poor reimbursement rates over lunch. Because there is a great deal of competition in their area, therapists often compete based on fees, and clients tend to go toward the lowest-fee practitioners. Each of the three CSWs says she is considering leaving the field. They consider their options for assisting one another in building successful practices in such an environment. Legally and ethically, they could:

    a. Set matching minimum fees, hoping that this will become the standard for their area.
    b. Form a grassroots movement of therapists called "Keep it 100," asking all therapists in the area to set a minimum fee of at least $100 an hour.
    c. Form a group practice to negotiate on rates with insurance companies as a single corporate entity rather than three individual practitioners.
    d. Work together to lower their fees temporarily, in hopes that this will put at least some competitors out of business. Then raise fees to a more acceptable level.

Practice Test

58. A military family in treatment with a CSW for four months comes into session appearing dazed, as the mother has learned she will be deployed to Germany in a matter of weeks. The family will be moving with her and will need to discontinue treatment immediately, they say, even though the treatment is incomplete. The CSW should:

   a. Discuss the transition, consider increasing the frequency of sessions in the remaining weeks, and encourage the family to continue therapy with a local provider during the deployment.
   b. Empower the father to delay the deployment, discuss the possibility of transition, and consider adding individual sessions with the mother.
   c. Assess for substance abuse, discuss the transition, and offer to provide online therapy during the deployment.
   d. Consider the deployment a "pause" rather than an ending of therapy, and encourage the family to continue treatment once they return.

59. A CSW with a full-time caseload finds herself on the edge of burnout. She notices she is becoming less empathetic and more combative with clients, and frequently arrives at the office in the morning still tired from the day before. A colleague she respects greatly refers her a complex case. The CSW should:

   a. Discontinue or temporarily pause treatment with some of her better-functioning clients in order to take the referral.
   b. Take the referral without changing any aspects of treatment for her other clients, and take other steps to manage her burnout.
   c. Decline the referral, and consider reducing her overall caseload.
   d. Accept the referral on a short-term basis, agreeing only to two sessions with the client in order to better assess their needs.

60. A CSW working with an individual client notices that the client has not paid for the last four sessions. The CSW discusses it with the client in session, and the client promises to pay their bill. The client then no-shows for their next three scheduled appointments. The CSW should:

   a. Offer the client a payment plan, discontinue treatment, and refer to low-fee services.
   b. Offer the client a payment plan, refer to low-fee services, and increase the frequency of contact until the bill is paid.
   c. Refer to low-fee services, and contact a responsible family member who may be able to assist with payment, without revealing any clinical information.
   d. Refer to low-fee services, and contact the client's employer to request a wage garnishment until the bill is paid, without revealing any clinical information.

61. A CSW is deeply concerned about her young adult client, who has been gradually weaning herself off of mood stabilizing medication. The client's doctor advised against the change, and the client has begun exhibiting risk-taking behavior including high-stakes gambling, experimentation with psychedelic drugs, and running barefoot on a freeway. In session, the client says she is planning her suicide, and that she has bought a gun. The CSW should:

   a. Assess the client's history.
   b. Move toward hospitalization.
   c. Contact the client's physician.
   d. Understand the suicidality as a side effect of discontinuing the medication.

62. The father of a CSW's adult client calls the therapist to say that the client is planning to kill the client's stepmother. The CSW does not have a Release of Information to speak to the father about the client. The father says that he fears the client is on his way now to the stepmother's home with a weapon. The father provides the stepmother's address and phone number. The CSW should:

 a. Not provide any information to the father, and contact police.
 b. Not provide any information to the father or to law enforcement.
 c. Not provide any information to the father, and attempt to contact the client.
 d. Not provide any information to the father, and attempt to send medical personnel to the stepmother's house.

63. A couple is receiving services together by court order, after an incident of intimate partner violence led to their children being temporarily removed from the home. Though the couple is making progress on co-parenting and conflict management in therapy, they have chosen to divorce. The court orders the CSW to provide a copy of the treatment record, and the CSW is uncomfortable disclosing to the court that he diagnosed one partner with Bipolar Disorder. The CSW should:

 a. Assert privilege on behalf of the clients.
 b. Contact the clients to determine their wishes.
 c. Provide the court a copy of the treatment record.
 d. Deny the court's request.

64. A CSW is running a therapy group for adults abused as children. Given the sensitive nature of the group, the CSW wants to begin with a discussion about privacy. Group members ask the CSW whether they can share information they learn in the group with their significant others at home. The most appropriate course of action would be for the CSW to:

   a. Remind group members of their legal obligation to keep information confidential.
   b. Discuss with the group why privacy is important to the success of the group process.
   c. Remind group members of their ethical obligation to keep information confidential.
   d. Discuss with the group what they believe the appropriate rules should be around such disclosures, as well as the consequences for violations of those rules.

65. A CSW is consulting with the physician who sent a young couple to the CSW for couple therapy. Both partners in the couple are struggling with symptoms of anxiety. The physician provides the CSW with useful information on the couple's medications and their possible side effects. The CSW offers the physician useful information on the progression of the couple's symptoms. Toward the end of the conversation, the physician asks whether the older partner in the couple is "still wearing that same brown sweater twice a week." The CSW should:

   a. Answer the question.
   b. Politely decline to answer the question, as it is not relevant to the consultation.
   c. Request a release from both partners to provide this type of information.
   d. Gently scold the physician for asking a question outside of their scope of practice.

Practice Test

66. After a family session where a family's 15-year-old daughter believed the CSW sided with the mother instead of the daughter, the daughter comes to the next session wearing earbuds she refuses to take out, and demanding an apology from the CSW. The CSW should:

   a. Consider whether the daughter is correct, and if appropriate, offer an apology.
   b. Side with the mother again, reinforcing the appropriate power hierarchy in the family.
   c. Refuse to go on with therapy until the 15-year-old removes her earbuds.
   d. Demand an apology from the 15-year-old.

67. A CSW has a client who lives on a boat three months of the year, as a commercial fisherman. During that time, he comes back to shore one day a week, and sees the CSW on that day. The client is relatively poor, and asks the CSW whether he can pay for services in fresh salmon. The client says he may need to discontinue treatment otherwise. The CSW frequently eats salmon, and so is familiar with the fair market value of the fish. Which of the following statements of the CSW's responsibilities is correct?

   a. The CSW should provide services pro bono, rather than accepting payment in fish.
   b. If the CSW chooses to go ahead with the barter agreement, the value of the fish should approximate the fee generally charged for therapy, and there should be a clear contract.
   c. The CSW should refer the client to a low-fee or no-fee clinic rather than accepting salmon as payment.
   d. The CSW should consider whether other clients would also want to pay for therapy through the products they make or services they provide.

68. A CSW suffers a serious illness, and a colleague steps in to take over the CSW's ongoing clients until the CSW can return to practice. The CSW agrees to continue handling billing and to review the colleague's session notes to keep up with what is happening while she is recovering. Some of the CSW's ongoing clients pay for sessions through their health insurance. However, the colleague (who is also a licensed CSW in private practice) is not on any insurance panels. The CSW should:

   a. Continue to submit insurance billing listing herself as the treatment provider.
   b. Continue to submit insurance billing listing the colleague as the treatment provider and herself as the supervisor.
   c. Either directly or through the colleague, inform clients of the difference in panel status and arrange alternate payment or referrals as needed.
   d. Defer to the colleague to negotiate fees independently, and otherwise presume that the CSW's typical business practices will be followed.

69. A CSW working with an adolescent client encourages one of the client's teachers to attend sessions that will focus on the adolescent's behavior in school. While the teacher's presence is at first helpful, the teacher asks to continue coming to the sessions, and it is clear to the CSW that the client is finding the teacher's presence gradually more intrusive and uncomfortable. The CSW should:

   a. Clarify the teacher's role in treatment, and ask the client whether they would like to continue having the teacher in session.
   b. Ask the client whether they would like to continue having the teacher in session, and remind the teacher of the limits to confidentiality.
   c. Ask the client to contact the school and request that the teacher be removed from the therapy sessions.
   d. Remind the client of the goals of therapy and the reasons for the teacher's presence in session.

Practice Test

70. An older woman who has been seeing a CSW for seven months storms out of session after her therapist started the session some 30 minutes late. The CSW attempted to explain that another client had been in crisis, but the woman cut off the CSW, saying that the delay was disrespectful of her time. A few days later the client calls the CSW saying she will not come back for future sessions and requesting a copy of the treatment record be sent to her. The CSW should:

   a. Insist that the client come in for an additional session to discuss her hurt feelings, and provide a copy of the treatment record.
   b. Apologize for the delay, offer to discuss it further, provide options for other treatment providers, and provide a copy of the treatment record.
   c. Provide a copy of the treatment record, and consider whether the client's display was simply a way of resolving cognitive dissonance about the need to end treatment.
   d. Provide options for other treatment providers, and inform the client that the CSW will forward the treatment record to the new provider of the client's choosing, in order to ensure that the client does remain in therapy.

71. A 14-year-old client who has consented for treatment independently is involved in a juvenile court case after being repeatedly caught stealing. The prosecuting attorney sends the CSW a subpoena requesting records of the client's therapy. The client expresses nervousness about their records being used against them in court. The CSW should:

   a. Contact the parents to determine their wishes, and respond to the subpoena accordingly.
   b. Use the CSW's clinical judgment to determine whether releasing the records would be beneficial to the minor, and respond to the subpoena accordingly.
   c. Assert privilege on behalf of the minor.
   d. Assert privilege on behalf of the parents.

72. A CSW who has been in private practice for five years decides to raise her fees. Which of the following is true?

   a. The CSW may raise fees for new clients going forward, but cannot change fees for ongoing clients.
   b. The CSW must provide at least 90 days notice to all clients for any changes in fees.
   c. The CSW cannot raise fees for existing clients more than 50% in one year.
   d. The CSW may raise fees for both new and ongoing clients, if she provides adequate notice to existing clients.

73. A CSW is concluding short-term treatment with a casting director for a production company that is interested in developing reality television shows about therapists. The client asks whether the CSW might be willing to be considered for one of the company's shows that will be casting in a few months. The client would not be involved in the casting decision, and would not inform others at the company that he had been in therapy with the CSW. The CSW should:

   a. Politely refuse the offer, as the casting decision would be made less than two years after the conclusion of therapy.
   b. Politely refuse the offer, as it would be a prohibited dual relationship.
   c. Consider the offer and inquire as to what the client's ongoing role in the show would be.
   d. Consider the offer under the condition that the client disclose the therapeutic relationship.

Practice Test

74. A family tells their therapist that they keep their 5-year-old son, who is not yet in school, locked in a small room for about 20 hours of each day for his own protection. The parents report that the son has severe birth defects and sensory processing difficulties, and cannot manage social situations or significant stimulus. The parents worry that their efforts to protect him are only worsening his developmental struggles, but see no other choice. The school-age children in the family describe the son jokingly as "the monster in the closet." The therapist should:

　　a. Discuss why the family describes the child as a "monster."
　　b. Report suspected child abuse.
　　c. Ask the parents to bring the child to the next session for the CSW to assess his physical development.
　　d. Assess the parental relationship.

75. A CSW advertises her solo private practice on a professionally-designed web site. The site uses stock photography of a modern, spacious office building, and a group of seasoned professionals holding clipboards. The CSW hopes the design of the web site and the photography it includes will bring an air of professionalism and sophistication to her practice, which she attempts to carry forward in her professional demeanor. Her web site:

　　a. Is likely to mislead prospective clients into believing she is part of a successful group practice.
　　b. Is not expected to be a fully factual representation of her practice.
　　c. Is acceptable so long as the text on the site is accurate.
　　d. Can be effectively balanced by full disclosure at the first session that she is in individual practice.

- STOP HERE -
END OF TEST

Practice Test
Answers and Rationales

Practice Test Answers and Rationales

1. A CSW has a new client who explains during the intake session that she had a hard time coming into therapy. The client says that her previous therapist asked her to go on a date with him at their termination session. She refused, and has not spoken with the former therapist again, but the experience left her skeptical of therapists generally. Legally, the CSW must:

- a. **Incorrect.** Report the other therapist's actions to the BBS. *The CSW could report the other therapist to the BBS, if the client signed a release of information allowing them to do so -- but it would be better for the client to report directly.*
- b. **Incorrect.** Confront the other therapist on their behavior. *The CSW has no legal obligation to confront the other therapist, and doing so in the absence of a release of information from the client would be a breach of confidentiality.*
- c. **Incorrect.** Provide the client a copy of the brochure "Professional Therapy Never Includes Sex." *Providing the "Professional Therapy Never Includes Sex" brochure would be a legal obligation if the client reported having had a sexual relationship. However, such a relationship never began.*
- d. **CORRECT.** Maintain the client's confidentiality. *None of the other options are an actual legal obligation in these circumstances.*

2. An adult client who has been seeing a CSW in therapy for six months asks the CSW for a copy of her treatment record. Because the CSW has documented that she suspects the client is being dishonest in her denials of recent drug use, the CSW worries that sharing the file would harm the therapeutic relationship. The most appropriate course of action for the CSW would be to:

   a. **Incorrect.** Turn over the records as required by law, and use it as an opportunity to address the client's possible substance use. *CSWs are not required to turn over requested records if the CSW believes the release would be harmful to the client.*
   b. **Incorrect.** Provide the client with a partial copy of the file, leaving out the suspicion of recent drug use. *While providing a treatment summary is legal and often appropriate, simply providing a partial copy of the file and leaving out the suspicion of drug use is not an option under the law. It may even be considered fraudulent if it is presented as if it were the complete record.*
   c. **CORRECT.** Refuse to turn over the records, offer a treatment summary instead, and inform the client that if she wishes, she can select a neutral therapist to review the file. *The CSW has good reason to believe that releasing the full treatment record could harm the therapeutic relationship and thus harm the client. Under the law, the CSW is allowed to offer a treatment summary instead. Further, when a CSW refuses to release records due to the risk of harm, the CSW must also inform the client of their right to a third-party review of the record by another therapist.*
   d. **Incorrect.** Submit the client's request, and the CSW's reason for refusing, to a district judge for review. *Turning over the records to a judge in the absence of a release of information from the client would be a breach of confidentiality.*

Practice Test Answers and Rationales

3. A group therapy client informs other group members that she has opened a bakery, and is willing to provide the other group members with a discount on purchases there. The client extends this offer to the CSW who facilitates the group, and clarifies that this is simply a way of saying "thank you" for running the group; the client does not expect any special treatment in return. The CSW must:

   a. **Incorrect.** Politely refuse the offer. *The CSW is not prohibited by state law or professional ethical codes from accepting the gift. The word "must" in the question is key – the CSW **may** refuse the offer if they choose, but they do not have to.*
   b. **CORRECT.** Consider the clinical and cultural implications of accepting or rejecting the offer. *The NASW Code of Ethics does not directly mention gifts at all, but these considerations would still be vital to determining whether the therapeutic relationship would be compromised.*
   c. **Incorrect.** Determine whether the value of the discount would be more than $25. *Current ethical guidelines do not limit a CSW's ability to receive gifts based on the monetary value of the gift.*
   d. **Incorrect.** Discourage group members from using the discount they have been offered. *While the CSW may be wise to have a discussion with the group to clarify that there is no expectation of a return favor, the CSW is not obligated to discourage the group from using the discount they have been offered.*

4. A CSW receives a subpoena from the attorney for an Italian restaurant where a client of the CSW formerly worked. The subpoena requests the client's complete clinical record, and notes that the client is suing the restaurant over the client's firing. The client claims that the firing was discriminatory and caused damage to her mental health. How should the CSW respond to the subpoena?

   a. **Incorrect.** Contact the client, determine her wishes, and encourage her to allow the records to be released now since the situation is an exception to confidentiality. *While an exception to privilege does apply when someone sues another party and makes their mental or emotional state an issue in the lawsuit, advising the client on a legal matter such as this would likely be considered outside the CSW's scope of practice.*
   b. **CORRECT.** Contact the client, determine her wishes, and assert privilege if she desires. *An exception to privilege may apply because of the lawsuit, but that is for a judge to determine if the client objects to the records being released.*
   c. **Incorrect.** Contact the court, assert privilege, and do not respond directly to the restaurant's attorney since a private subpoena is not a court order. *While a private subpoena is indeed not the same as a court order, simply failing to respond may land the therapist in trouble with the court. It would be better to respond by asserting privilege, if that is the client's desire -- and knowing the client's wishes would require first contacting the client, not the court.*
   d. **Incorrect.** Contact the court, assert privilege, and respond to the subpoena by saying that records cannot be released without the client's signed consent. *It is the client, not the court, that should be contacted first. You can then act in accordance with her wishes, at least until the court makes a determination as to whether an exception to privilege applies. The remainder of this option is also incorrect as there are exceptions to privilege (including one that likely applies here) that would allow records to be released absent the client's consent, if a judge determines this to be appropriate.*

Practice Test Answers and Rationales

5. A CSW is seeing a family for an intake session. The family includes three foster girls, ages 16, 13, and 10. During individual interviews with each of the children, they all reveal that they are currently in sexual relationships. The 16-year-old received treatment for a sexually transmitted disease a year ago after catching it from her then-17-year-old boyfriend. The 13-year-old says that she is having sex with her 14-year-old boyfriend. And the 10-year-old tells you that she is pregnant, though she will not reveal anything about the age or identity of the father. Which of these relationships must be reported as child abuse?

   a. **Incorrect.** All three children's relationships are reportable. *See rationale below.*
   b. **Incorrect.** The 16-year-old's relationship and the 10-year-old's relationship are reportable. *See rationale below.*
   c. **CORRECT.** Only the 13-year-old's relationship is reportable. *See rationale below.*
   d. **Incorrect.** Only the 10-year-old's relationship is reportable. *See rationale below.*

The correct answer is C. Neither sexually transmitted disease (the 16-year-old) nor pregnancy (the 10-year-old) are sufficient evidence in and of themselves to reasonably suspect child abuse. While the age of the 10-year-old is certainly troubling, if her partner were of similar chronological and maturational age, their sexual activity may not be reportable. The age combination of the 16-year-old and 17-year-old suggests that their consensual intercourse is also not reportable. Only the 13-year-old, by engaging in consensual intercourse with a 14-year-old, is in a sexual relationship that qualifies as an automatic report under the law.

6. The 59-year-old client of a CSW calls her therapist from the hospital for a planned check-in conversation. The client tells the therapist she has been hospitalized for a severe respiratory infection and is likely to remain as an inpatient in the hospital for at least another two weeks. She also expresses a belief that hospital staff are stealing her belongings. The CSW should:

   a. **Incorrect.** Maintain the client's confidentiality. *See rationale below.*
   b. **Incorrect.** Report the client's belief to hospital staff. *See rationale below.*
   c. **CORRECT.** Report the client's accusation as suspected dependent adult abuse. *See rationale below.*
   d. **Incorrect.** Presume the client's accusation is a side effect of the pain medication she is likely receiving, and take no further action. *See rationale below.*

The correct answer is C. Any inpatient in a 24-hour health care facility (such as a hospital) is automatically considered a dependent adult under state law. And unlike the rules for child abuse reporting, when an elder or dependent adult directly reports a behavior that would qualify as abuse, the therapist is generally obligated to report it. (There is a narrow carve-out in the law for elders or dependent adults with medical concerns that would impact their ability to recall events.) Because the client is making a direct accusation of financial abuse, this must be reported.

Practice Test Answers and Rationales

7. A client reports to her therapist, a CSW, that the client's antidepressant medication does not appear to be having a positive effect even after eight weeks of her taking the prescribed dosage. The CSW should:

    a. **Incorrect.** Encourage the client to request a medication change. *See rationale below.*
    b. **Incorrect.** Encourage the client to request a higher dosage to achieve the intended effect. *See rationale below.*
    c. **CORRECT.** Encourage the client to consult with her physician. *See rationale below.*
    d. **Incorrect.** Encourage the client to consider discontinuing the medication and focusing on efforts to improve her depressive symptoms through therapy. *See rationale below.*

The correct answer is C. Any other response choice would be advising on medication, which is outside of the CSW scope of practice. CSWs can only guide clients back to their physician to address medication-related concerns.

8. A CSW is involved on a treatment team for a county social service agency. The CSW grows frustrated that the CSW's suggestions are rarely implemented by the team. An appropriate course of action would be for the CSW to:

   a. **CORRECT.** Seek advice from colleagues about handling treatment team dynamics. *The NASW Code of Ethics encourages CSWs to seek advice when such consultation is in clients' best interests.*
   b. **Incorrect.** Temporarily stop providing input into team decisions until the CSW can better understand why previous suggestions have not been implemented. *Social workers are ethically obligated to be actively involved in interdisciplinary treatment teams. Stopping participation, even temporarily, would violate this standard.*
   c. **Incorrect.** In the interest of transparency, directly inform clients of the CSW's recommendations, including those that the team has rejected. *This could undermine treatment decisions made by the team, and places clients in a difficult position. It does not live up to social workers' requirement to work collaboratively with colleagues. To the degree that the CSW seeks to have clients take the CSW's side, this could be considered exploitation of the client.*
   d. **Incorrect.** Demand that the team implement the CSW's suggestions to promote the well-being of clients. *It is not collaborative for one member of a treatment team to make demands. Even if the team's decisions raised ethical concerns – which is not indicated by the question stem – making demands of the team is unlikely to resolve those concerns effectively.*

Practice Test Answers and Rationales

9. A CSW is being interviewed for a podcast. The interviewers ask about her training and clinical work, and repeatedly refer to her as "Doctor," even though her highest degree is a master's degree. The CSW should:

    a. **Incorrect.** End the interview and ask that it not be released. *Ending the interview would be a drastic and probably unnecessary step.*
    b. **Incorrect.** No action is called for, as the interview does not qualify as advertising. *Because the interview discussed her clinical work, the interview may be considered advertising. A correction is needed to ensure listeners are not misled as to the CSW's education.*
    c. **Incorrect.** Continue the interview, and afterward, remind the interviewer of her proper title. *Reminding the interviewer afterward of her proper title might mean that the incorrect title is used many more times during the recording, misleading listeners.*
    d. **CORRECT.** Politely correct the interviewers, and ensure that the correction is included on any edited version of the interview used in the podcast. *The NASW Code of Ethics requires social workers to correct misinformation about their qualifications.*

10. A family from Cambodia is seeing a CSW for family therapy. During a family session, the father tells the therapist that he sometimes disciplines his 15-year-old son the same way the father had been disciplined in Cambodia when he was young: With lashes across his back, using a stick. The mother voices her objection to this form of discipline, and notes that on multiple occasions the son was left bleeding and crying. The most appropriate action for the CSW would be to:

a. **Incorrect.** Consider the cultural elements involved and inform the clients that such discipline may not be accepted in the US. *While CSWs must consider cultural influences when designing and implementing treatment, the reporting standards for physical abuse are written to be as objective as possible: If the intentional striking of a child leaves an injury, it is reportable as physical abuse. Failing to report suspected abuse is a legal violation.*

b. **CORRECT.** Report suspected physical abuse to the local child protective service agency. *If the intentional striking of a child leaves an injury, it is reportable as physical abuse. It is up to the local child protective service agency to determine whether and how to involve cultural factors in their response to the abuse.*

c. **Incorrect.** Remind the family of the limits of confidentiality and ask whether there are any photos of the son's injuries. *Asking for photos places the CSW in the role of investigator rather than treating clinician.*

d. **Incorrect.** Consider the cultural elements involved and research common Cambodian disciplinary practices to determine whether the behavior is consistent with cultural norms. *While CSWs should consider cultural influences when designing and implementing treatment, the reporting standards for physical abuse are written to be as objective as possible: If the intentional striking of a child leaves an injury, it is reportable as physical abuse. Failing to report suspected abuse is a legal violation.*

Practice Test Answers and Rationales

11. A CSW shopping for clothing approaches the checkout counter and observes that the only worker at the cash register is a client of hers. The CSW should:

 a. **CORRECT.** Make her purchases as she normally would, behaving like an ordinary customer unless the client chooses to behave in a more familiar manner. *While this does place the CSW in a dual relationship, such relationships are not prohibited. CSWs are asked to avoid those avoidable dual or multiple relationships that may increase the risk of exploitation or impair clinical judgment. Neither appears to be the case here, and behaving as a normal customer protects the client's confidentiality.*
 b. **Incorrect.** Ask to speak with the store's manager, and explain that she needs to be checked out by a different worker, without providing any information on the reason why. *This would simply serve to call attention to the multiple relationship, potentially doing more harm than good.*
 c. **Incorrect.** Leave the store. *This arguably does no harm, but is not necessary. If the client had noticed the therapist in the store, the client may be insulted or hurt by the therapist simply walking out, harming the therapeutic relationship.*
 d. **Incorrect.** Inform the client that, in order to protect the client's privacy, she will return to the store on a different day. *This would simply serve to call attention to the multiple relationship, potentially doing more harm than good.*

12. A 70-year-old client tells a CSW that the client had been under-medicated for several months while living at a nursing home in Florida the prior year. The CSW asks how the client knows this, and the client says that her prescription specifically noted that her medication should be given twice a day, but she received it only once each day. The CSW believes the client has good cognitive functioning. The CSW should:

  a. **Incorrect.** Report suspected elder abuse to the CSW's local adult protective service agency. *Because she was living in Florida at the time the under-medication occurred, she was not an elder adult as California defines it.*
  b. **Incorrect.** Report suspected elder abuse to the adult protective service agency local to the nursing home in Florida. *Because she was living in Florida at the time the under-medication occurred, she was not an elder adult as California defines it.*
  c. **CORRECT.** Encourage the client to report what happened to the appropriate adult protective service agency in Florida. *The therapist is not obligated to report this under California law, which includes California residency in the definition of an elder adult.*
  d. **Incorrect.** Encourage the client to document the events for a possible civil lawsuit against the nursing home in Florida. *This amounts to providing legal advice to the client, which is outside the CSW scope of practice.*

Practice Test Answers and Rationales

13. A 14-year-old girl presents for therapy at a local mental health clinic, where a CSW is assigned to her case. During a screening interview, the girl tells the CSW that she is struggling with anxiety around her schoolwork and social relationships. She goes on to say that she plans to pay for therapy on her own and would prefer that her parents not know she is in therapy. The CSW should:

   a. **CORRECT.** Assess the girl's ability to participate intelligently in therapy and determine whether notifying the parents would be damaging. *Minors 12 and older can independently consent for treatment if the therapist considers them mature enough to participate intelligently. No adult needs to consent on their behalf. This law also requires therapists to contact the parents unless doing so would be damaging.*
   b. **Incorrect.** Determine whether notifying the parents would be damaging and determine what adult can consent for the girl's therapy. *Minors 12 and older can independently consent for treatment if the therapist considers them mature enough to participate intelligently. No adult needs to consent on their behalf.*
   c. **Incorrect.** Assess the girl's ability to participate intelligently in treatment and inform her that even when seen under her own consent, her parents may have the right to access her records if they become aware she is in therapy. *When a minor consents for their own therapy, the parents do not have a right to records of treatment.*
   d. **Incorrect.** Determine whether notifying the parents would be damaging and determine whether notifying the girl's school would be damaging. *Notifying the school without the client's permission could be a breach of confidentiality.*

14. A CSW provided therapy to a 16-year-old boy for several months with his parents' consent. A few months later, the CSW receives a subpoena from the attorney for a classmate of the boy. The classmate accused the client of physical assault, and the classmate's family is suing to recover medical expenses. The subpoena requests complete records of the boy's treatment. The CSW attempts to contact the client and his parents but is unsuccessful. The CSW should:

   a. **Incorrect.** Wait to respond to the subpoena until the CSW is able to determine how the client would like the CSW to respond. *Failing to respond to a subpoena may land the CSW in trouble with the court.*
   b. **Incorrect.** Wait to respond to the subpoena until the CSW is able to determine how the parents would like the CSW to respond. *Failing to respond to a subpoena may land the CSW in trouble with the court.*
   c. **CORRECT.** Respond to the subpoena by asserting privilege, and continue attempts to contact the client and his parents. *When clients cannot be reached to determine their preferred response to a subpoena, asserting privilege on their behalf is a reasonable default position to take.*
   d. **Incorrect.** Acknowledge the exception to privilege, turn over the client's records, and inform the client and his family as soon as possible. *It is up to a judge, and not the therapist, to determine whether an exception to privilege applies.*

Practice Test Answers and Rationales

15. A former client calls the CSW who had treated her two years earlier. The former client verbally requests that the CSW forward her file to her new therapist in a different state. The former client confirms her identity using her social security number and is able to identify specific topics of the prior therapy, leaving the CSW confident in the identity of the caller. The CSW should:

   a. **Incorrect.** Take down the information for the new therapist and forward the file as the client requested. *This option does not leave the therapist with any documentation of the request at all.*
   b. **Incorrect.** Take down the information for the new therapist, contact that therapist, and have that therapist complete a written records request. *The request for records should come from the client, not from the new treatment provider.*
   c. **Incorrect.** Take down the information for the new therapist, and inform the former client that she will need to request that the records be released directly to her. She can then forward the file to the new therapist if she so chooses. *With the client's permission, records can be transferred directly to the new treatment provider. They do not need to first go through the client.*
   d. **CORRECT.** Take down the information for the new therapist, and send the former client appropriate paperwork to request in writing that her file be released. *The client should provide permission in writing for the release of their records.*

Preparing for the California Clinical Social Work Law & Ethics Exam

16. A potential client with partial paralysis contacts a CSW and asks whether he may receive therapy by phone for his symptoms of depression. The CSW assesses the potential client by phone and determines he is appropriate for phone-based services. Legally, the CSW must:

   a. **CORRECT.** Obtain consent for phone-based services and inform the potential client of the possible risks and benefits. *These are current legal requirements.*
   b. **Incorrect.** Obtain consent in writing for phone-based services and inform the potential client that such services are currently considered experimental in nature. *Consent for telehealth can be provided verbally under state law, and does not need to be in writing.*
   c. **Incorrect.** Assess the client in person at least once before moving to phone-based services. *While assessing the client in person first may be helpful, it is not currently a legal or ethical requirement.*
   d. **Incorrect.** Assess the client in person and identify the closest hospital emergency room to the client, in case of emergency. *While assessing the client in person first may be helpful, it is not currently a legal or ethical requirement.*

Practice Test Answers and Rationales

17. A social worker has been working with a family for several sessions and plans a session where the entire family will participate in a ceremony relieving the oldest daughter of the responsibility she has taken on as a co-parent. Shortly before the session, the mother informs the CSW that she will be away on a business trip and asks whether she can participate in the session by phone or videoconferencing. The mother's frequent absences are part of the reason why the daughter felt obligated to take on parenting tasks. The social worker should:

    a. **Incorrect.** Contact the BBS to see whether the CSW can include the mother in session while she is on her trip. *The BBS does not provide legal advice, and even asking the question may require providing information that is confidential.*
    b. **Incorrect.** Include the mother in the session and in the ceremony via phone or videoconference, and clarify that her involvement is consultation rather than therapy. *Simply calling the mother's involvement consultation does not make it something different from therapy. This is especially true considering that the entire purpose of her presence in session is to be involved in a therapeutic intervention that the CSW designed.*
    c. **CORRECT.** Refuse the mother's request and reschedule the ceremony for a time she can attend in person. *CSWs are required to carefully assess whether telemedicine services are appropriate in a given case. Here, the mother's absence would likely have a major impact on the planned ceremony; having her participate by phone or videoconference rather than in person appears likely to impact the effectiveness of the intervention.*
    d. **Incorrect.** Contact the other family members to see whether they believe including the mother would be legally and ethically appropriate. *While the family may be able to offer useful clinical feedback on this question, it is not the role of the family to resolve the CSW's legal and ethical concerns.*

18. A walk-in client at a local counseling center presents with moderate suicidal ideation and racing thoughts. The front desk worker at the clinic tells an available CSW that the client should be seen immediately, and that the clinic manager has approved skipping the usual intake paperwork to get the client in to see the CSW as quickly as possible, as the client has verbally agreed to be seen. Legally, the CSW should:

a. **CORRECT.** Inform the client of the fee for services, and the basis on which the fee is computed, prior to beginning treatment. *Informing the client of the fee and the basis on which it was computed are legal obligations. While the client is experiencing moderate suicidal ideation, there is no further evidence in the vignette to suggest that the CSW could not take the minimal amount of time needed to fulfill these obligations, or that doing so would somehow be dangerous.*
b. **Incorrect.** Demand that the client complete the full standard intake paperwork for the clinic prior to beginning treatment. *This may not be necessary, as the standard paperwork may include a great deal of information gathering that is not legally or ethically required and that may be reasonably deprioritized to assess for safety.*
c. **Incorrect.** Inform the client of the limits of confidentiality prior to beginning treatment. *This is an ethical, rather than a legal, obligation.*
d. **Incorrect.** Demand that the clinic manager provide approval in writing for skipping the usual intake paperwork, in order to reduce the CSW's potential liability. *While the CSW should document their permission from the clinic manager, and to have it in writing might be particularly helpful, this is not a legal requirement, and placing such a demand ahead of caring for the client is to place the CSW's interests ahead of those of the client.*

Practice Test Answers and Rationales

19. A CSW working primarily with Jewish clients learns from one such client that the client, as well as two other clients of the CSW, attend the same synagogue. The three had discussed their therapist over lunch one day, describing traits that they did and did not like about the CSW's work. The CSW should:

   a. **CORRECT.** Consider whether the clients' discussion of each other in therapy would impair clinical judgment or increase the risk of exploitation. *Prior to taking additional steps, the CSW should consider whether they are engaging in an inappropriate multiple relationship. Potential impairment of clinical judgment and potential exploitation are the factors to examine, in accordance with professional ethical codes.*
   b. **Incorrect.** Remind all three clients of the limits of confidentiality. *This would be appropriate when considering instances where the therapist may legally or ethically break confidentiality, but does not address the clients' protection of their own confidentiality outside of session.*
   c. **Incorrect.** Encourage all three clients to share as little from their therapeutic work as possible, to preserve their independent therapeutic relationships with the CSW. *Restricting them from doing sharing information about their therapy is neither necessary nor appropriate, as it would interfere with client autonomy in determining what information from therapy they wish to share with others.*
   d. **Incorrect.** Ask that the clients not discuss anything about each other or their shared synagogue in session, focusing instead on the issues and relationships unique to each client. *Restricting them from discussing the others in therapy may prevent them from talking about important events in their social and spiritual lives, hindering treatment.*

Preparing for the California Clinical Social Work Law & Ethics Exam

20. An associate CSW has been struggling with a difficult family case. The associate's supervisor suggests that the associate record video of future sessions so that the associate and supervisor can together review what happens in session. The associate is reluctant to record sessions, fearing that the parents in the family might feel embarrassed. The associate CSW is required to:

   a. **Incorrect.** Remind the clients that, because the associate is under supervision, video recording of sessions is a common and accepted practice. *While this may be a common and accepted practice, pushing the clients in this way may lead them to believe that they do not have the ability to refuse recording.*
   b. **CORRECT.** Obtain specific consent for recording from each adult family member prior to recording sessions. *This is required by the NASW Code of Ethics.*
   c. **Incorrect.** Comply with the supervisor's request even if the family would prefer to not be recorded, as the associate is working under the supervisor's license. *Consent for taping cannot be forced upon the clients. They should be fully informed of the risks and benefits, and choose on their own.*
   d. **Incorrect.** Remind the clients of the limits of confidentiality prior to recording sessions. *While doing so is helpful, it is not required, and does not resolve the associate's reluctance to tape.*

Practice Test Answers and Rationales

21. A 20-year-old woman seeks the services of a CSW. The woman explains to the therapist that she would like individual therapy to help her get along better with her college roommate. Ethically, the CSW should:

   a. **Incorrect.** Refer the client to at least three local therapists qualified to treat the problem, as it is outside the CSW's scope of practice. *Individual treatment for interpersonal problems is well within the CSW scope of practice.*
   b. **Incorrect.** Refer the client to at least three local therapists qualified to treat the problem, as it is outside the CSW's scope of competence. *While scope of competence is determined by one's individual level of training and experience, all CSWs should have the training and experience minimally necessary to treat this case.*
   c. **CORRECT.** Inform the client of the potential risks and benefits of treatment. *This is a routine part of the informed consent process.*
   d. **Incorrect.** Inform the client that she will need to bring the roommate into therapy with her. *Bringing the roommate into treatment may be clinically appropriate, and some CSWs may even require it, but it is not an ethical obligation.*

22. Two clients in a therapy group have become friends outside of the group. They often arrive to group together and appear to share inside jokes during the group. Other group members express concern to the CSW running the group that they are being made fun of or that what they share in the group may come up between these two friends outside of group. The CSW should:

   a. **CORRECT.** Encourage concerned members to express their concerns in the group. *This best preserves client autonomy and the integrity of the group process. It also would invite a conversation about how group members should handle confidentiality among each other.*
   b. **Incorrect.** Reassure concerned members that ethically the two friends cannot share information from the group outside of the group context. *Ethics are the responsibility of the therapist running the group. While social workers should discuss client roles and obligations to one another early in the group process, clients do not have an ethical responsibility to each other. The CSW also cannot guarantee that group members will respect the rules of the group.*
   c. **Incorrect.** Remove one of the two friends from the group and refer them to another group. *This would be punitive and could do more harm than good. It would be an overreaction to the situation of two group members becoming friends.*
   d. **Incorrect.** Demand that the two members who have become friends explain to the group the nature of their friendship and any group-related conversations they have had outside of the group. *Forcing client disclosure to other group members goes against client autonomy and could be considered a misuse of the therapist's power. Clients have the right to disclose only that information they want to disclose to the group.*

Practice Test Answers and Rationales

23. An individual client acknowledges to her therapist (a CSW) that she lied on the CSW's intake form and actually does have several past suicide attempts in her history. She says she is not feeling suicidal now, though she has recently experienced the ending of a romantic relationship and the death of a distant relative. Legally, the CSW should:

   a. **Incorrect.** Complete a No Harm Contract with the client. *No Harm Contracts have largely fallen out of favor, replaced by safety plans; either way, such a response here would likely be considered inadequate to the client's level of risk.*
   b. **Incorrect.** Discontinue therapy and refer the client to a higher level of care, as she is high risk. *Discontinuing therapy is not a legal requirement and may be clinically harmful, leaving the client with the lesson that they will be punished if they openly discuss their history of suicidality.*
   c. **Incorrect.** Initiate the process of involuntary hospitalization. *While the client does pose an elevated level of risk, the fact that she denies current suicidality means that an attempt to initiate involuntary hospitalization would likely be considered a breach of confidentiality -- and that hospitals would likely turn her away to keep room available for higher-risk patients who are more actively suicidal.*
   d. **CORRECT.** Assess further and break confidentiality if required to resolve any threat of suicide. *CSWs are legally obligated to take steps necessary to prevent a threatened suicide, and may break confidentiality if necessary as part of that process.*

24. A CSW is working with an individual client who was recently fired in a way the client experienced as humiliating. The client tells the therapist that he intends to go this weekend to the office building where he had worked, ensure no people are present in the building, and as long as no people would be endangered, burn the building down. "I know their insurance would cover the losses," the client says, "I just want to make a point." Legally, the CSW must:

a. **Incorrect.** Report the threat to the business to ensure that all current employees are protected. *See rationale below.*
b. **Incorrect.** Report the threat to local police, providing minimal additional information about how the CSW knows of the threat. *See rationale below.*
c. **Incorrect.** Warn the client that unless he takes back his threat, the CSW must break confidentiality to protect the employees of the business. *See rationale below.*
d. **CORRECT.** No specific action is required. *See rationale below.*

The correct answer is D. The client's clear statements that he does not intend to hurt any people in the building make it difficult to argue that he poses an imminent danger to reasonably identifiable victims (A, B, and C all rely on such danger). While section 1024 of the Evidence Code presents an exception to privilege for threats to property (and this has been interpreted by some to mean that confidentiality may be breached for such threats), there is no *obligation* to report threats to property. (Recall that the question asked for what the CSW *must* do, not what they *could* do.)

Practice Test Answers and Rationales

25. A CSW in private practice is concluding her last session of the day. After the session ends, the client pays her fee by credit card and schedules their next meeting, and both CSW and client walk out of the building where the practice is located. There, the CSW realizes she has had forgotten her wallet and does not have the cash to cover her usual bus fare to get home. The client offers cash to pay the therapist's bus fare. When the CSW initially refuses the offer, the client suggests that the money simply be credited toward the next session's fee. Ethically, the therapist should:

a. **CORRECT.** Politely refuse the offer and work to find another way to get home. *Even under the guise of a "partial prepayment," this situation would clearly amount to the CSW borrowing money from the client – a multiple relationship that can quickly become problematic.*
b. **Incorrect.** Accept the offer under the condition that it is a prepayment of part of the next session fee. *There is no stated reason why this client might normally prepay a few dollars toward the next session's fee; the intention would still appear to be to loan money to the therapist.*
c. **Incorrect.** Offer to immediately provide a partial session just a few minutes in length, for which the client could pay a small amount of cash for professional services. *Immediately providing a partial session for cash would be serving the therapist's needs, not the client's.*
d. **Incorrect.** Accept the offer, keep the transaction separate from payments for therapy, and repay the client in cash at the beginning of the next session. *This option records the transaction as a loan, and borrowing money from a client is likely to be considereda violation of the standards protecting clients from possible exploitation in multiple relationships.*

26. A CSW covered by HIPAA plans to move her office approximately five miles and has hired a moving company to transport all of her office furniture, supplies, and equipment. How should the therapist address the file cabinets that contain hard copy client files?

   a. **Incorrect.** Hire an additional security contractor approved by HIPAA to oversee the move and ensure records are transported without security breaches. *Hiring a second contractor for the purposes of security is unnecessary. It also would not resolve the problem of the moving company not having a Business Associate Agreement in place.*
   b. **CORRECT.** Ask the moving company to provide a Business Associate Agreement establishing that they will abide by the rules HIPAA sets forth regarding privacy and security of client data. *Any contractor who will have access to protected health information must provide a Business Associate Agreement establishing that they will also follow the privacy rules in the law.*
   c. **Incorrect.** Remove all files and transport them herself, as HIPAA requires that contractors not be given access to client records without client consent. *Under HIPAA, it is acceptable for contractors to have access to protected information, but any contractor who will have access to protected health information must provide a Business Associate Agreement establishing that they will also follow the privacy rules in the law.*
   d. **Incorrect.** Demand that every employee of the moving company that will be working on her move sign a privacy statement agreeing to follow strict security standards. *Having employees of the company sign privacy statements would not be sufficient protection.*

Practice Test Answers and Rationales

27. A client who has expressed great concern about anyone knowing she is in therapy passes out in the middle of a session. The CSW the client was seeing is able to wake her long enough to learn that she has recently been struggling with illness and has pain from a neck injury, and the CSW knows from the client's intake paperwork that she has a blood disorder. The CSW should:

　　a. **Incorrect.** Stay with the client and continue attempting to wake her. *Passing out mid-session may be indicative of a medical emergency. Absent other information, it should be treated as an emergency.*
　　b. **Incorrect.** Call 911 and transport the client outside of the office into a public area to protect her privacy. *Calling 911 is appropriate, but attempting to transport the client is not, particularly given her known neck injury. Further, it is difficult to argue that moving the client to a public area from a private one would protect her privacy.*
　　c. **Incorrect.** Call 911 and summon paramedics without providing any information about the client or her illness. *Paramedics may need information on the woman's recent illness and blood disorder in order to treat her appropriately. It is acceptable to share this information with other health care providers in an emergency, and the CSW can do so without revealing anything about the woman's therapy.*
　　d. **CORRECT.** Call 911, summon paramedics, and inform them of the client's medical issues. *CSWs are allowed to share medical information in an emergency situation, and the CSW in this instance can do so without revealing any information about the client's therapy.*

Preparing for the California Clinical Social Work Law & Ethics Exam

28. A CSW who is new to the community seeks to build her referral base so that she can grow her practice. For those colleagues who refer clients to her, she calls the colleague (without revealing any information about the client) and offers to buy the colleague lunch to say thanks and engage in professional networking. An established CSW in the community receives such an offer from the new CSW after referring a client to the new CSW. How should the established CSW respond?

   a. **CORRECT.** Accept the invitation under the condition that they each agree to pay their own bill. *As long as the established CSW is not receiving any form of payment, it would be acceptable to join the new CSW for lunch or coffee.*
   b. **Incorrect.** Decline the invitation and report the new CSW to the BBS. *It would be acceptable to decline the invitation, but reporting to the BBS is not justified. Ethical obligations include assisting colleagues and respecting their confidences; it would be better to discuss with the new CSW the risks inherent in their offer.*
   c. **Incorrect.** Accept the invitation under the condition that no client information will be discussed. *Having the new CSW pay for her lunch would amount to receiving payment for referrals, which is specifically prohibited by state law and the NASW Code of Ethics.*
   d. **Incorrect.** Accept the invitation and request a release of information from the client allowing the established CSW to discuss the case with the new CSW. *Having the new CSW pay for her lunch would amount to receiving payment for referrals, which is specifically prohibited by state law and the NASW Code of Ethics.*

Practice Test Answers and Rationales

29. A CSW is surprised to see that her new client did not complete the CSW's standard informed consent paperwork in the waiting room prior to their scheduled session. The CSW brings the client into her therapy office, where the client says that he can only read and write in Spanish. He speaks English fluently, and says he prefers that his therapy sessions be in English. The CSW only speaks and writes in English. Ethically, the therapist should:

a. **Incorrect.** Have a verbal conversation to establish informed consent, and have the client sign the informed consent document. *There is no requirement or ethical preference that informed consent be provided via signature; it is enough to document informed consent in session notes.*
b. **CORRECT.** Have a verbal conversation to establish informed consent, and document that conversation in session notes. *Informed consent can be provided verbally and documented appropriately.*
c. **Incorrect.** Provide a Spanish language translation of her informed consent documents as soon as possible, for the client to read and sign. *While a Spanish language version of the informed consent may be useful to have, since the CSW does not read in Spanish, there may be issues with translation that the CSW would not be aware of. The client may then have a different understanding of what they have consented to than the therapist would.*
d. **Incorrect.** Have a verbal conversation about informed consent, and offer to provide a Spanish language translation of her informed consent documents as soon as possible. *Since the client understands English well, the conversation is likely to be sufficient. Since the CSW does not read in Spanish, there may be issues with translation that the CSW would not be aware of. The client may then have a different understanding of what they have consented to than the therapist would.*

30. A CSW learns that his individual client, who is being seen for symptoms of Bipolar Disorder, is also interested in attending couple therapy with her spouse. The client asks the CSW whether the couple could see the CSW together for couple therapy separately from her individual sessions, and says she is willing to sign a release form such that information from her individual sessions could be discussed in couple therapy and vice versa. Ethically, the CSW should:

   a. **CORRECT.** Continue individual treatment with the client and refer out for the couple therapy. *This preserves continuity of care for individual treatment and keeps the CSW out of a potential conflict of interests that would result from serving the client in multiple roles.*
   b. **Incorrect.** Continue individual treatment with the client and begin concurrent couple therapy, utilizing a separate file with a separate treatment plan. *Even with a release in place and a clearly different treatment plan, the therapist is likely to be more aligned with the partner being seen individually as well. Better to refer out for couple therapy to a therapist who will be more neutral.*
   c. **Incorrect.** Conduct a screening interview with the couple, as well as with each partner individually, to assess whether adding couple therapy to the client's existing treatment plan would be appropriate. *While adding couple treatment may be clinically appropriate, it should not be added with the same therapist because of the pre-existing (and continuing) relationship with one partner.*
   d. **Incorrect.** Discontinue the individual treatment in order to begin couple treatment, with the client's release in place to allow for material from the individual sessions to be discussed in couple work. *Discontinuing individual treatment prematurely does not appear likely to be in the best interests of the client.*

Practice Test Answers and Rationales

31. A CSW is working with a family where the parents are in the process of getting a divorce and are arguing over custody of their two children. Therapy has focused on maintaining effective co-parenting, as neither parent wants an extended court battle. Because the CSW knows the family well and has seen both parents interacting with the children, the parents ask the CSW to submit a letter to the court with the CSW's clinical evaluation of each of their parenting skills. The best course of action for the CSW would be to:

- a. **Incorrect.** Obtain a release from all family members, and send the letter to the court, emphasizing that the evaluative statements should not be used to draw conclusions about custody. *See rationale below.*
- b. **Incorrect.** Obtain a release from all family members, and send the letter to the court, offering specific recommendations for custody based on the CSW's work with the family and based on the CSW's knowledge of the wishes of the children. *See rationale below.*
- c. **Incorrect.** Obtain a release from all family members, and engage in a process of testing and evaluation to draw objective conclusions before completing the letter. *See rationale below.*
- d. **CORRECT.** Refuse to send the letter. *See rationale below.*

The correct answer is D. The NASW Code of Ethics requires social workers to clarify their role and avoid conflicts of interest. The parents in this case are asking the CSW, who has been in the treatment provider role, to also take on an evaluative stance. If the CSW were to do so, the parents would likely be less forthcoming in the future about any struggles they experienced in parenting. Options (A), (B), and (C) all place the CSW in an evaluator position that should be avoided if the CSW has provided clinical treatment.

Preparing for the California Clinical Social Work Law & Ethics Exam

32. An adult client tells a CSW that the client's 89-year-old mother is in hospice care. The client goes on to say that the hospice staff have been screening the mother's mail and phone calls, as they are concerned that she would fall prey to financial scammers who target the elderly. The client tells the CSW that the mother has severe dementia and that the client believes the screening of mail and phone calls is appropriate. The client also says the staff has never refused him access to his mother. The CSW should:

    a. **Incorrect.** Obtain a release from the client, contact the hospice directly, and gather more information about the mother's diagnosis and the need for mail and calls to be screened. *Even if there were evidence of abuse, the CSW should not take on an investigator role.*

    b. **Incorrect.** Report suspected elder abuse to the CSW's local adult protective service agency. *There is no evidence of abuse here.*

    c. **CORRECT.** Maintain the client's confidentiality. *It appears to the client, and as presented to the CSW, that the hospice's actions in screening mail and phone calls are appropriate. Further, they are not refusing the client access to his mother.*

    d. **Incorrect.** Empower the client to gather more information on the mother's diagnosis and the need for mail and calls to be screened, and ask the client to bring that information to a future session for the client and the CSW to review together. *There does not appear to be reason for the CSW to suggest concerns to the client, nor is there reason for the CSW and client to investigate together.*

Practice Test Answers and Rationales

33. A CSW learns that her client's adopted son was recently involved in a series of hit-and-run accidents. At present, law enforcement is investigating but does not know who is responsible. The client expresses fear of all possible outcomes; if the police determine it was her son, the son will likely go to jail. If the police do not determine it was her son, the son may continue with his risky and damaging behavior. The client says she does not want to turn her son in. Considering her legal and ethical obligations, the CSW should:

a. **Incorrect.** Report the son to law enforcement as a potential danger to others. *The CSW does not have enough information to justify such a report. There is nothing to indicate that the son's behavior represents an imminent danger.*
b. **Incorrect.** Anonymously report the son's actions to law enforcement, without revealing the name of the therapist or the client, and without revealing how the CSW came to know the information. *For the CSW to decide to report would be to breach confidentiality; even if the CSW does not reveal the source of the information, she would be sharing confidential information learned from the client in therapy.*
c. **Incorrect.** Encourage the client to report the son to law enforcement to reduce the risk that he will harm others in the future. *Encouraging the client to report the son could be seen as interfering with the client's autonomy, placing the therapist's values above the client's.*
d. **CORRECT.** Discuss the client's feelings in greater detail and examine the risks and benefits of various possible courses of action while maintaining the client's confidentiality. *There is no reason here for the therapist to break confidentiality. The focus then becomes addressing how the client should handle the information she has.*

34. A CSW is distressed to learn that a former client has posted a detailed account of the client's therapy online in the form of an article. While the article is mostly positive, it mentions the CSW by name and includes some incorrect information about the CSW's qualifications. The CSW notices that it is possible to leave comments on the article. The CSW should:

    a. **Incorrect.** Post a comment in response to the article, thanking the author while also correcting the errors. *Clients do not give up their right to confidentiality even when they voluntarily discuss their therapy. Acknowledging the social worker-client relationship in the absence of a release to do so can be considered a breach of confidentiality even if the client has already done so.*

    b. **Incorrect.** Contact the site owners to ask that the article be taken down, without specifying whether the writer was actually a client. *While the CSW should correct the errors, asking that the article be taken down is overstepping. Respecting client autonomy includes respecting their right to share their experiences in therapy as they see fit. There is nothing here to indicate that taking down the article would be necessary or helpful.*

    c. **CORRECT.** Contact the former client directly to encourage them to correct the article. *CSWs have an ethical obligation to correct misinformation about their qualifications once they discover it. In this case, contacting the former client directly appears to be the most appropriate means to do so..*

    d. **Incorrect.** No action is called for. *While the CSW must be respectful of the client's autonomy and their right to share therapy experiences as they see fit, the CSW also has an obligation to take reasonable steps to correct misinformation about their qualifications.*

Practice Test Answers and Rationales

35. A CSW is working with an individual client who is employed in the movie industry. The client is emotionally unstable following a breakup. The client informs the CSW that the client will be travelling out of state for the next three weeks to work on a film, and asks whether the CSW can continue to work with the client by phone during that time. The CSW should first:

   a. **Incorrect.** Assess the severity of the client's symptoms to determine whether phone therapy is appropriate, and if so, proceed with phone sessions. *There is no point in doing the assessment if the CSW is not authorized to provide services in the state where the client will be.*
   b. **CORRECT.** Determine whether they have the requisite qualifications to practice in the state to which the client is travelling. *Phone sessions are only an option if the therapist is legally authorized to provide services in the state to which the client will be travelling. If the therapist is also licensed in that state, or if the state has a carve-out in their licensure law allowing for short-term continuation of care with an out-of-state therapist, then the phone sessions requested here are a possibility, pending further assessment.*
   c. **Incorrect.** Determine the client's state of residency. *Residency does not matter. The BBS, like most state licensure boards, considers the physical location of the client at the time of service as where the therapy takes place (and, thus, where the therapist needs to be licensed or otherwise authorized to provide care).*
   d. **Incorrect.** Inquire with the BBS as to the appropriateness and legality of phone sessions for this client. *The BBS cannot provide legal advice and may not know current licensing requirements for all other states. It would be a more appropriate step to check with the licensing board of the state where the client will be, to see what the rules there are.*

36. A polyamorous couple experiencing difficulty in their sexual relationship presents for therapy with a CSW who believes sexual activity outside of a monogamous relationship is inappropriate and harmful. The couple does not believe that their sexual relationships outside of their own relationship are causing their sexual problems with each other. Ethically, the CSW should:

   a. **Incorrect.** Seek to address underlying emotional issues that may be impacting the couple's sexual relationship, so as to improve the relationship without directly discussing the couple's other partners. *While the couple certainly may be correct in their reporting that polyamory is not a problem for them, avoiding discussion of it in therapy is likely to quickly become awkward given that they are there to address couple relationship issues.*
   b. **CORRECT.** Refer the couple to a therapist who does not share the CSW's belief. *The therapist's belief is closely related to the issue for which the couple is seeking treatment, and is likely to interfere with that treatment.*
   c. **Incorrect.** Inform the clients in advance of her belief, allowing the clients to determine whether they would like to continue therapy with her. *It is the therapist's responsibility, not the client's, to determine when the therapist's values are likely to interfere with effective care.*
   d. **Incorrect.** Begin therapy by explaining her belief and the underlying research, and explaining that the couple's theory that their polyamory is not related to their own sexual difficulty is unlikely to be true. *This explanation serves only to defend the therapist's belief and presupposes the cause of the couple's problems.*

Practice Test Answers and Rationales

37. A CSW's client confesses to her that he is struggling with guilt over his involvement in three recent gang-related murders. Two adults were killed: one was a rival gang member, the other was an innocent bystander. The third victim was also a rival gang member, and was just 17 years old. The client tells the CSW that he does not believe he or the others in his gang will be caught, but this is only worsening his guilt. How should the CSW handle her legal obligations surrounding confidentiality?

   a. **Incorrect.** Break confidentiality for the three murders and work with law enforcement to warn other members of the rival gang. *CSWs generally have no obligation to report past crimes, and doing so could be considered a breach of confidentiality.*
   b. **Incorrect.** Break confidentiality for the murder of the bystander and work with law enforcement to warn other members of the rival gang. *CSWs generally have no obligation to report past crimes, and doing so could be considered a breach of confidentiality.*
   c. **CORRECT.** Break confidentiality for the murder of the 17-year-old, and otherwise maintain confidentiality. *Child abuse must be reported, and in this case the murder of the 17-year-old qualifies as child abuse. Child abuse must be reported even when it resulted in the death of the victim.*
   d. **Incorrect.** Maintain the client's confidentiality for all past acts, and encourage him to consider self-reporting to law enforcement if necessary to resolve his guilt. *The murder of the 17-year-old qualifies as child abuse. It must be reported, so the CSW cannot legally maintain confidentiality for "all past acts."*

38. A CSW finds herself becoming increasingly blunt and even harsh with a client who is overweight and experiencing depression. The CSW realizes she is judging the client for the client's weight and her apparent lack of interest in resolving any of the personal or relational struggles that the CSW believes are perpetuating the client's depressive symptoms. The client continues attending therapy and reporting attempts to complete homework assigned by the therapist, but without improvement. The CSW should:

   a. **CORRECT.** Seek consultation and attempt to repair the therapeutic relationship. *The client's continued efforts suggest that the therapeutic relationship has not been damaged beyond repair. The CSW and client are both best served by the CSW seeking to understand and correct her personal biases while continuing to treat.*
   b. **Incorrect.** Seek consultation and refer the client to a therapist who does not share the CSW's weight bias. *A therapist bias does not always require a referral. In some instances it is better to continue treatment while managing the bias and repairing the relationship. In this case, the client's continued efforts suggest that the relationship can be preserved.*
   c. **Incorrect.** Refer the client out and seek additional training to recognize and not blame the client for common correlates to depression. *A therapist bias does not always require a referral. In some instances it is better to continue treatment while managing the bias and repairing the relationship. In this case, the client's continued efforts suggest that the relationship can be preserved.*
   d. **Incorrect.** Refer the client out as it does not appear that therapy has a reasonable likelihood of success. *Nothing in the question stem suggests that therapy is hopeless. It is possible that the CSW's efforts to address her own biases and repair the therapeutic relationship could lead to meaningful gains.*

Practice Test Answers and Rationales

39. A CSW is close to successful termination with a father who has been in treatment for 15 sessions. The father expresses his gratitude to the CSW, and says he would like to find a way to help families with similar needs. The CSW is aware of an online discussion group where the father could share his experience in therapy, steering potential clients toward the CSW and offering hope to families experiencing similar problems to the ones his own family had experienced at the beginning of therapy. Ethically, the CSW should:

a. **Incorrect.** Encourage the father to share his experience in the discussion group, including both positive and negative components, and including the CSW's name so that other participants know where they can receive confidential help. *Asking for the CSW's name to be included would amount to solicitation of a testimonial, which is ethically prohibited.*
b. **CORRECT.** Thank the father for his work in therapy, and discuss potential benefits and risks of several potential means by which the father could help similar families. *Confidentiality is the client's right, and they are free to share information from the therapy as they see fit.*
c. **Incorrect.** Thank the father for his work in therapy, and discourage him from publicly sharing his experience in the interest of confidentiality. *Since the father would like to use the family's experience to help others, it does not make sense to discourage him from doing so. This would arguably interfere with his autonomy.*
d. **Incorrect.** Encourage the father to share his experience in the discussion group but to do so anonymously, only naming the CSW if he chooses to do so. *Unless the therapist can foresee a specific harm to the client from doing so, it does not make sense to discourage the client from using his name if he wishes.*

40. A mother arrives late for her therapy session and is enraged. She reports that she just spent an hour dealing with police, who came to the grocery store where her car was parked and were about to break a window when she returned to the car and stopped them. The police, she said, rudely lectured her about the infant son she had left in the car while she was grocery shopping. While the car was in sunlight, it was only about 80 degrees out at the time and she had been away from the car for less than 20 minutes, she said. The CSW should:

   a. **Incorrect.** Explore the mother's feelings of anger and shame. *Exploring her feelings may be clinically useful, but is not required; a report of suspected child neglect is required.*
   b. **Incorrect.** Assess whether the son had suffered any harm. *Unlike with other forms of child abuse, children do not need to have suffered any actual injuries to qualify as having been neglected.*
   c. **Incorrect.** Ask for a Release of Information and offer to contact police directly to follow up. *Contacting police to follow up on the incident is offered here without a rationale, so it is unclear whether this would serve any meaningful clinical purpose. To the degree that it may help with the decision of reporting, it places the CSW in an investigator role.*
   d. **CORRECT.** Report suspected child neglect. *Leaving an infant alone in a car in direct sunlight presents significant danger to the child. Even if the child did not suffer actual harm, a report is justified.*

Practice Test Answers and Rationales

41. A CSW is interested in conducting research on her clients, in an effort to determine whether a new form of treatment developed by the CSW is superior to existing treatments. Because the CSW already has access to the client files and would be reporting statistics on her treatment results, without specifics of any individual cases, she prepares to conduct an analysis of cases she has closed over the prior year. She hopes to publish the results of her research in a prominent journal. Ethically, the CSW should:

   a. **CORRECT.** Contact those former clients, inform them of the risks and benefits of involvement in the research, and determine their willingness to have their file included as one of those analyzed. *The NASW Code of Ethics requires that research participants provide informed consent for their participation, including information about risks and benefits and the opportunity to choose not to participate.*
   b. **Incorrect.** Take steps to protect the confidentiality of individual cases, but include all cases from the prior year in her analysis to eliminate possible selection bias. *While there is reasonable concern that those clients who choose not to participate might skew results, participants' rights outweigh concerns about possible selection bias.*
   c. **Incorrect.** Contact those former clients to let them know that their files have been included in her research. *Simply informing them after the fact that they were included would not meet professional standards. It neglects an informed consent process for research and does not give the clients the opportunity to choose against being part of that research.*
   d. **Incorrect.** Because she is working with archival data that will be reported in aggregate, no action is required. *Even though results will be reported in aggregate, the CSW's clients had not been informed that they were also research participants. They must be given the opportunity to choose whether to be involved in the research. While the NASW ethics code allows some exceptions for archival research, this is only appropriate when obtaining consent is not feasible.*

42. A client is aware of a local wellness center that is soon to be put up for sale. The client tells her therapist, a CSW, about the business and how much she would like to join the CSW in buying it. She presents a detailed proposal that would have them end their therapy relationship so that they could become investment partners. The CSW should:

   a. **Incorrect.** Carefully consider the risks and benefits associated with the potential investment. *While what is proposed in the question would be, technically, a business venture with a former patient, termination should be based on sound clinical judgment and not on a financial opportunity arising. The CSW should not accept this offer regardless of the balance of risks and benefits associated with the investment.*
   b. **CORRECT.** Remind the client of the boundaries of the therapy relationship. *Engaging in a business venture with a client is a problematic dual relationship, and ending therapy to engage in a business relationship is prohibited.*
   c. **Incorrect.** Inform the client that the CSW will only consider terminating therapy if it is clinically appropriate, and that any potential investment partnership could only be discussed once the therapeutic relationship has ended. *Ending therapy to engage in a business relationship is prohibited. Better for the CSW to remain in a clinical role here.*
   d. **Incorrect.** Thank the client for her consideration in bringing the opportunity to the CSW, and suggest other possible investment partners. *Suggesting other investment partners is not consistent with serving in a clinical role.*

Practice Test Answers and Rationales

43. A CSW has recently completed his hours of supervised experience and successfully completed the examination process, earning full licensure as a CSW. He is in the process of leaving the clinic where he worked as an associate, and setting up a private practice. In his last two weeks at the clinic, he tells his clients about his planned move. Many of his clients ask to see him at his new private practice once it opens rather than continuing treatment with a different therapist at the clinic. The CSW should:

   a. **Incorrect.** Inform his supervisor of those clients' plans, make copies of their records, and take the originals to his new practice, leaving the copies with the agency. *The therapist could not simply take files (or copies of files) without permission.*
   b. **Incorrect.** Ensure that all fees for continuing clients will be the same at his private practice as they were at the clinic. *He is not obligated to apply the same fee structure as the clinic did. Rather, like any change in treatment provider (and moving from a clinic to a private practice is a change), the new provider is obligated to inform clients of the fee and the basis on which it is computed.*
   c. **CORRECT.** Ask each client who is planning to continue at his private practice to sign a Release of Information, authorizing the clinic to release the client's records to the CSW. *Records belong to the employer, not the clinician. The client would need to specifically allow the employer to release records to the CSW.*
   d. **Incorrect.** Politely refuse to see clients at his new practice, as these clients are clients of the clinic and must continue treatment there. *Clients also have autonomy to choose their treatment providers, so it does not make sense to restrict them from continuing with a therapist they know and trust.*

Preparing for the California Clinical Social Work Law & Ethics Exam

44. A CSW develops a friendly relationship with a physician who works in an adjacent building. The CSW asks the physician to refer any patients who need mental health services to the CSW, and provides a stack of $25 coupons the physician can give to patients to encourage them to contact the CSW. The CSW would apply that $25 toward the fee for the first session. The CSW should:

a. **Incorrect.** Maintain the referral relationship, but discontinue the use of coupons. *There is nothing inherently illegal or unethical about the use of coupons that would necessitate their being discontinued.*
b. **Incorrect.** Discontinue the referral relationship, and market directly to prospective clients. *Having a referral network of trusted professionals helps ensure that clients' clinical needs are met; it is fine to market to other providers as well as to prospective clients. Marketing does not always need to be done directly.*
c. **CORRECT.** Ensure that new clients referred from the physician are fully aware of all fees to be charged. *Disclosure of fees is a legal requirement.*
d. **Incorrect.** Maintain the referral relationship, discontinue the use of coupons, ensure all clients pay the same fee for services, and thank the physician for referrals by directly paying the physician $25 for each new client she refers. *There is nothing inherently illegal or unethical about the use of coupons that would necessitate their being discontinued. Also, payments to other providers for referrals are legally and ethically prohibited.*

Practice Test Answers and Rationales

45. A Caucasian CSW receives a phone call from a prospective new client couple. The couple reports that they moved to the US from India three years ago, and they would like to come to therapy to work on communication difficulty in their marriage. The CSW strives to maintain strong awareness of cultural issues, but has never worked with anyone from India before. The best course of action for the CSW would be to:

a. **Incorrect.** Refer the couple to a therapist of Indian descent. *Referring the couple out would be discrimination based on national origin.*
b. **Incorrect.** Encourage the clients to educate the CSW about Indian culture and customs. *Relying solely on the clients to educate the therapist on cultural issues is not sufficient; the CSW is expected to do additional work on their own to develop competence where it is lacking.*
c. **CORRECT.** Seek resources and consultation to become familiar with Indian culture and customs, and to understand how Indian clients typically present in therapy. *This best summarizes the CSW's responsibilities. Understanding typical client presentation based on the client culture does not mean the CSW should or would assume that the particular case will match cultural norms, but at least provides a useful reference point for assessment.*
d. **Incorrect.** Wait until the clients come in for an initial assessment to determine whether meaningful cultural differences exist. *Waiting until the clients come in leaves the CSW vulnerable to their own blind spots related to cultural difference, and may lead to incorrect assessment of the couple.*

46. A famous actor contacts a CSW seeking help with his anxiety. Because he is so well-known, the actor expresses concern that the fact that he is in therapy could be "leaked" to the media, making it harder for him to be cast in desirable roles. He asks the CSW whether he can pay solely in cash so that the CSW will not have financial records, and he asks the CSW to keep records for treatment under a fake name that the actor would use when signing all treatment-related documents. How should the CSW respond?

    a. **CORRECT.** Refuse the requests. *CSWs are bound to keep treatment records that are accurate and reflect sound clinical judgment. The actor's requests would violate these standards.*

    b. **Incorrect.** Refuse the request to keep records under a fake name, but allow the client to sign all documentation using whatever fake name they choose. *This may violate the requirement that CSWs keep accurate records. It also would create difficulty if the CSW relied on those signed documents as evidence of an informed consent process.*

    c. **Incorrect.** Honor the request to keep treatment records under a fake name, but refuse the request to not keep financial records. *CSWs are bound to keep records that are accurate. Using a fake name would violate that requirement.*

    d. **Incorrect.** Agree to both requests to protect the client's privacy while otherwise maintaining the terms of treatment. *CSWs are bound to keep records that are accurate and consistent with the standards of the profession.*

Practice Test Answers and Rationales

47. A client mandated for treatment by his county probation office returns to therapy after a six-month absence. He informs the CSW that he needs records of his progress in treatment sent to his probation officer before his next court date, and provides a Release of Information allowing those records to be sent. However, he carries a balance due of more than $500 from sessions he attended but did not pay for prior to being absent from therapy. The CSW should:

    a. **Incorrect.** Continue with treatment at a reduced fee, and refuse to turn over records until at least a portion of the balance is paid. *Ethically a CSW must provide reasonable access to records. It is likely to be considered unethical to refuse to turn over records simply because the client owes money.*

    b. **Incorrect.** Continue with treatment at a reduced fee, and refuse to turn over records until the outstanding balance is paid in full. *Ethically a CSW must provide reasonable access to records. It is likely to be considered unethical to refuse to turn over records simply because the client owes money.*

    c. **CORRECT.** Consider terminating the client if he will be unable to pay his balance, and turn over records to the probation officer. *Termination for non-payment of fees can be ethical. The client as requested and authorized the release of records.*

    d. **Incorrect.** Consider terminating the client if he will be unable to pay his balance, and notify the probation officer of the outstanding balance. *The probation officer is not involved in the payment agreement between therapist and client; disclosing the client's balance is not necessary or in the client's best interests.*

48. A CSW conducting her fourth home visit with a high-conflict family in poverty sees suitcases in their living room. When the CSW asks about the suitcases, the family's 15-year-old daughter announces that she is moving out, with plans to live with friends. She is not willing to provide the names of those friends or any other information to her family or to the CSW. The CSW should:

   a. **Incorrect.** Report the case to the CSW's local child protective service agency, as the 15-year-old is at high risk for abuse or neglect. *There is no evidence here to support reasonable suspicion of abuse or neglect.*
   b. **CORRECT.** Attempt to gain more information about the daughter's plans. *The presence of suitcases observable to the therapist may simply be the 15-year-old's way of attempting to communicate a warning to her family. It does not, in and of itself, trigger any specific legal or ethical responsibilities.*
   c. **Incorrect.** Consider hospitalizing the daughter as a protective measure. *There is no evidence of danger to self or others.*
   d. **Incorrect.** Focus clinical attention on the parents, noting that they will be the ones around to continue clinical work, and terminate with the 15-year-old. *Abruptly discontinuing treatment with her could be considered abandonment.*

Practice Test Answers and Rationales

49. A CSW working in a middle school setting is confronted by a parent who is upset that the CSW has not filed a child abuse report over the bullying her daughter has faced. The daughter is regularly taunted by other girls at the school and has been injured in some shoving matches. Though the daughter has sought to avoid these fights and does not fight back, the CSW defends herself by noting that in each case the girl has been fighting with other girls around the same age and size. The daughter is a regular client of the CSW, and the mother has attended some sessions. The CSW should:

  a. **Incorrect.** Contact her local child protective service agency to report the mother for failing to protect her child. *It is not the mother's job to protect the child while the child is at school.*
  b. **CORRECT.** Contact her local child protective service agency to report physical abuse of the daughter. *While there is an exception to the physical abuse reporting standards when children engage in willful mutual combat ("a mutual affray between minors," according to section 11165.6 of the Penal Code), the fact that the girl here is seeking to avoid these fights is critical. It means that they cannot accurately be described as mutual. Even when the combatants are of similar age and size, if one is being pushed into combat against their will, it can qualify as physical abuse under the law.*
  c. **Incorrect.** Contact the school principal to discuss the mother's concerns. *This would raise confidentiality concerns and would not resolve the CSW's reporting responsibility.*
  d. **Incorrect.** Calmly explain to the mother why her daughter's injuries are not considered problematic. *This would not resolve the CSW's reporting responsibility (see the rationale above for response B).*

Preparing for the California Clinical Social Work Law & Ethics Exam

50. The individual client of a CSW tells the CSW that he recently took his 94-year-old grandfather, who has been suffering from dementia, on a fishing trip to a nearby lake in a California State Park. He had grown frustrated with the quality of care the grandfather had been receiving at his nursing home, which he said was not adequate to the grandfather's medical needs. He also wanted to give his grandfather "one last hurrah," as he was concerned the grandfather's death was just weeks away. He was angry that the nursing home staff had berated him upon their return for not notifying them he was taking the grandfather for the weekend. The CSW should:

a. **Incorrect.** Report the nursing home for inadequate care, and the client for kidnapping. *While the nursing home care may be inadequate, the simple fact that a family member describes it as such does not mean it is so, and it certainly does not mean the problems in care rise to the level of being abusive or neglectful. (Note that a direct report of suspected abuse* from the victim *generally triggers reporting responsibility for elder or dependent adult abuse.) Also see the rationale for response C below.*

b. **Incorrect.** Report the nursing home for inadequate care. *While the nursing home care may be inadequate, the simple fact that a family member describes it as such does not mean it is so, and it certainly does not mean the problems in care rise to the level of being abusive or neglectful.*

c. **Incorrect.** Report the client for kidnapping. *The simple fact that the client took his grandfather on a fishing trip does not mean the grandfather was kidnapped. The definition of kidnapping in elder abuse reporting law specifically requires that the victim have been taken outside of California.*

d. **CORRECT.** Ask the client to clarify how the nursing home's care is inadequate. *There is nothing reportable in this vignette. While the nursing home care may be inadequate, the simple fact that a family member describes it as such does not mean it is so, and it certainly does not mean the problems in care rise to the level of being abusive or neglectful. While the CSW does not want to take on the role of investigator, inquiring about the client's frustrations with his grandfather's care is clinically appropriate.*

Practice Test Answers and Rationales

51. During an unusually tense family session, a mother confronts a CSW on the CSW's recent filing of a written report of suspected child abuse. The mother feels violated and reports that she can no longer trust the CSW. Other family members attempt to calm the mother, but share her concerns. The CSW should:

- a. **Incorrect.** Discontinue treatment, as the therapeutic relationship has been irreparably compromised. *While there may have been damage to the therapeutic relationship, attempts to repair are appropriate before deciding that therapy is a lost cause.*
- b. **CORRECT.** Remind the family of the limits of confidentiality, and seek to regain the family's trust. *The ethics code reminds CSWs that circumstances may require multiple discussions of the limits of confidentiality.*
- c. **Incorrect.** In the interest of full disclosure, inform the mother that follow-up reports to the local child protective service agency may be necessary. *When written reports are filed, the therapist has discharged their responsibility by filing the report, and does not need to file follow-up reports unless new instances of abuse emerge.*
- d. **Incorrect.** Ask to speak to the other family members without the mother present, to determine whether there is an appropriate path forward for therapy. *Speaking to other family members without the mother present would likely only further her distrust of the CSW and harm the therapeutic relationship.*

52. A CSW who has had a long and successful career working primarily with high-powered business executives wants to write a tell-all book detailing the cases he saw in his practice and the lessons he learned from his clients, some of whom are well-known in the business and technology worlds. The best course of action for the CSW would be to:

   a. **Incorrect.** Wait at least seven years since the last professional contact with all clients, at which point their records are no longer confidential. *While records must be retained for at least seven years, they remain confidential forever.*
   b. **Incorrect.** Surrender his license and professional association membership prior to writing the book, so that no action can be taken against him for using client names. *Releasing confidential information remains against the law even after a license has been surrendered, so giving up the license would not protect the CSW from some legal actions.*
   c. **CORRECT.** Falsify any identifying information about each client he discusses. *When using clinical materials in a public forum, the NASW Code of Ethics requires that social workers not disclose any identifying information about clients without their consent.*
   d. **Incorrect.** Sell the book exclusively outside of California, to protect former clients from having friends and neighbors read about their clinical experiences. *Selling only outside of California would be difficult on a practical level, but more importantly, would still be releasing confidential information.*

Practice Test Answers and Rationales

53. A CSW worked with a woman in individual therapy for six months, focusing on treatment of depression symptoms following the client's messy divorce. The client improved significantly in therapy and terminated successfully. One year later, the CSW has been dating a man for two months when the CSW realizes the man is the ex-husband of the former client. The CSW should:

   a. **Incorrect.** Discontinue the romantic relationship. *The ex-husband is not a current or former client. The client terminated successfully. None of the standards surrounding social workers' sexual partners appear to apply here. There is reason to wonder whether the former client may wish to return to therapy in the future, and what the CSW should do in that instance. But that is not part of the question at hand.*
   b. **Incorrect.** Contact the former client to determine her wishes. Given the amount of time that has passed and the success of treatment, she is likely to give her blessing. *Contacting the former client inappropriately places the therapist's interests ahead of the former client's, and makes the former client responsible to some degree for the CSW's ethical decision-making.*
   c. **Incorrect.** Self-report to the BBS to seek their guidance on the most appropriate way to proceed. *The BBS does not serve in the role of ethics consultant. They enforce the legal standards of the profession. If the CSW is interested in an ethical opinion, they should contact NASW or other professional and legal resources.*
   d. **CORRECT.** No action is called for. *Because none of the ethical prohibitions regarding sexual relationships appear to apply here, the CSW is not obligated to any specific course of action.*

54. A CSW is studying a group therapy process for adolescents who have been victims of child abuse. The parents of one of the members of the group ask to have their 16-year-old child removed from the group and from the study, noting that they believe the group is making the child's trauma symptoms worse. The parents had been informed of this risk prior to agreeing to put their child in the study. The CSW should:

a. **Incorrect.** Remind the parents of the agreement they signed outlining the risks of the research, and attempt to convince them to keep their child in the group. *See rationale below.*
b. **Incorrect.** Remind the parents of the agreement they signed outlining the risks of the research, and leave the decision about participation up to the child. *See rationale below.*
c. **CORRECT.** Remove the child from the group, and take steps to resolve any negative impacts the group caused for the child. *See rationale below.*
d. **Incorrect.** Take steps to resolve any negative impacts the group caused for the child, and keep the child in the group based on the parents' initial agreement. *See rationale below.*

The correct answer is C. One of the rights of research participants is the right to withdraw participation at any time; with minors, this includes the right of parents to withdraw their child's participation. The fact that the parents signed an agreement at the beginning of the study, indicating that they understood the risks of the study, does not change their right to withdraw their child.

Practice Test Answers and Rationales

55. A CSW works across the street from a major software company's offices. The CSW begins advertising specifically to employees of the company, using the company's logo on the CSW's website and business cards to say that the CSW is "now proudly serving employees of" that company. One client, who works for the software company and had found the CSW through the website, asks about the relationship between the CSW and the software company. The CSW should:

- a. **Incorrect.** Clarify for the client that there is no formal relationship, and that the CSW simply enjoys working with employees of the company. *Clarifying this for one client who has been misled, while helpful, does not prevent others from being similarly misled by the CSW's advertising.*
- b. **CORRECT.** Change the website and business cards to not use the company's logo. *Use of the company's logo suggests an affiliation with the company that does not exist.*
- c. **Incorrect.** Seek to develop a more formal relationship with the company, including a contract to treat their employees. *The possible development of a more formal relationship with the company in the future does not make the CSW's advertising any less misleading in the present.*
- d. **Incorrect.** Change the website and business cards to indicate that the company's logo is a registered trademark used with permission. *Providing an indication that the company logo is trademarked does not solve the problem of the marketing material being misleading. Also note that this response did not include the CSW actually obtaining that permission.*

56. A client comes to a CSW looking for treatment that her insurance will help pay for. The CSW has a waiting list for new clients. The CSW is the only CSW in the client's rural community, however, the CSW is aware of two counselors and one Psychologist in the community who may be able to treat the client immediately. The CSW should:

   a. **Incorrect.** Put the client on the CSW's waiting list. *Keeping the client on the CSW's waiting list when other qualified providers are available is putting the therapist's welfare above the client's.*
   b. **CORRECT.** Inform the client of the other local providers. *Clients generally have freedom of choice under insurance laws, meaning they can see whatever qualified treatment provider they choose. Of course, not all providers are "in-network" with insurers, but at a minimum the therapist should inform the client that the other providers in town may be able to see her more quickly and still have the treatment paid for.*
   c. **Incorrect.** Contact the insurance company to determine whether they generally pay for the services of LCSWs or Psychologists. *The client or the therapist could contact the insurance company to inquire about their reimbursement practices, though again, laws require that clients have freedom of choice as to their treatment providers.*
   d. **Incorrect.** Base all referral decisions exclusively on the client's diagnosis. *While the client's diagnosis is a factor in determining referrals, it is also appropriate to consider factors like waiting lists and insurance coverage.*

Practice Test Answers and Rationales

57. Three CSWs working in different private practices in the same city share their frustrations with poor pay and poor reimbursement rates over lunch. Because there is a great deal of competition in their area, therapists often compete based on fees, and clients tend to go toward the lowest-fee practitioners. Each of the three CSWs says she is considering leaving the field. They consider their options for assisting one another in building successful practices in such an environment. Legally and ethically, they could:

   a. **Incorrect.** Set matching minimum fees, hoping that this will become the standard for their area. *See rationale below.*
   b. **Incorrect.** Form a grassroots movement of therapists called "Keep it 100," asking all therapists in the area to set a minimum fee of at least $100 an hour. *See rationale below.*
   c. **CORRECT.** Form a group practice to negotiate on rates with insurance companies as a single corporate entity rather than three individual practitioners. *See rationale below.*
   d. **Incorrect.** Work together to lower their fees temporarily, in hopes that this will put at least some competitors out of business. Then raise fees to a more acceptable level. *See rationale below.*

The correct answer is C. All three of the other options would be considered anti-competitive behavior under antitrust law. CSWs in private practice are independent businesses and must compete with one another in the marketplace; jointly setting fees, regardless of whether they are set high (A) or low (D) or in the middle (B), is anti-competitive.

58. A military family in treatment with a CSW for four months comes into session appearing dazed, as the mother has learned she will be deployed to Germany in a matter of weeks. The family will be moving with her and will need to discontinue treatment immediately, they say, even though the treatment is incomplete. The CSW should:

   a. **CORRECT.** Discuss the transition, consider increasing the frequency of sessions in the remaining weeks, and encourage the family to continue therapy with a local provider during the deployment. *Given that their treatment is incomplete, it would be better for them to continue it with a local provider during the deployment than to simply wait out the deployment while family problems continue.*
   b. **Incorrect.** Empower the father to delay the deployment, discuss the possibility of transition, and consider adding individual sessions with the mother. *It is unlikely that the father could delay the deployment; even if he could, adding individual sessions while family sessions continue would be a potential conflict of interests.*
   c. **Incorrect.** Assess for substance abuse, discuss the transition, and offer to provide online therapy during the deployment. *There is nothing in the vignette to indicate heightened risk of substance abuse.*
   d. **Incorrect.** Consider the deployment a "pause" rather than an ending of therapy, and encourage the family to continue treatment once they return. *Given that their treatment is incomplete, it would be better for them to continue it with a local provider during the deployment than to simply wait out the deployment while family problems continue.*

Practice Test Answers and Rationales

59. A CSW with a full-time caseload finds herself on the edge of burnout. She notices she is becoming less empathetic and more combative with clients, and frequently arrives at the office in the morning still tired from the day before. A colleague she respects greatly refers her a complex case. The CSW should:

  a. **Incorrect.** Discontinue or temporarily pause treatment with some of her better-functioning clients in order to take the referral. *See rationale below.*
  b. **Incorrect.** Take the referral without changing any aspects of treatment for her other clients, and take other steps to manage her burnout. *See rationale below.*
  c. **CORRECT.** Decline the referral, and consider reducing her overall caseload. *See rationale below.*
  d. **Incorrect.** Accept the referral on a short-term basis, agreeing only to two sessions with the client in order to better assess their needs. *See rationale below.*

The correct answer is C. Interrupting treatment with other clients in order to take a new referral (A) may be considered abandonment of those existing clients, and is putting the therapist's needs above those of the clients. Maintaining the same caseload while adding a complex case (B) is likely to only worsen the CSW's burnout; she needs to recognize her limitations and not add to her workload. Accepting the referral on a short-term basis (D) is not likely to be in the best interests of a complex case, and does nothing to move toward resolving the burnout that may be impacting *all* of the CSW's caseload.

Preparing for the California Clinical Social Work Law & Ethics Exam

60. A CSW working with an individual client notices that the client has not paid for the last four sessions. The CSW discusses it with the client in session, and the client promises to pay their bill. The client then no-shows for their next three scheduled appointments. The CSW should:

   a. **CORRECT.** Offer the client a payment plan, discontinue treatment, and refer to low-fee services. *Discontinuation of treatment over unpaid balances can be ethically appropriate, under specific conditions.*
   b. **Incorrect.** Offer the client a payment plan, refer to low-fee services, and increase the frequency of contact until the bill is paid. *Increasing contacts over an unpaid bill may be perceived as punishment or harassment. The frequency of contact should be determined based on clinical needs, not financial standing.*
   c. **Incorrect.** Refer to low-fee services, and contact a responsible family member who may be able to assist with payment, without revealing any clinical information. *Contacting a family member would be a breach of confidentiality.*
   d. **Incorrect.** Refer to low-fee services, and contact the client's employer to request a wage garnishment until the bill is paid, without revealing any clinical information. *Contacting the employer would likely be a breach of confidentiality even if no clinical information is given.*

Practice Test Answers and Rationales

61. A CSW is deeply concerned about her young adult client, who has been gradually weaning herself off of mood stabilizing medication. The client's doctor advised against the change, and the client has begun exhibiting risk-taking behavior including high-stakes gambling, experimentation with psychedelic drugs, and running barefoot on a freeway. In session, the client says she is planning her suicide, and that she has bought a gun. The CSW should:

a. **Incorrect.** Assess the client's history. *Assessing the client's history is helpful but does not address the immediate danger.*
b. **CORRECT.** Move toward hospitalization. *There are several specific factors the CSW can point to here that suggest heightened immediate risk for suicide.*
c. **Incorrect.** Contact the client's physician. *Contacting the client's physician may help the CSW understand the effects of discontinuing the medication, but does not address the immediate risk for suicide.*
d. **Incorrect.** Understand the suicidality as a side effect of discontinuing the medication. *While it would take more information to know whether the suicidality is linked to the change in medication compliance, even if there is a direct causal link, simply understanding this does not reduce the risk to the client.*

62. The father of a CSW's adult client calls the therapist to say that the client is planning to kill the client's stepmother. The CSW does not have a Release of Information to speak to the father about the client. The father says that he fears the client is on his way now to the stepmother's home with a weapon. The father provides the stepmother's address and phone number. The CSW should:

   a. **CORRECT.** Not provide any information to the father, and contact police. *In the* Ewing v. Goldstein *case, California courts determined that third-party information can trigger a therapist's Tarasoff responsibilities. This is thus a situation where a therapist has a duty to protect the intended victim.*
   b. **Incorrect.** Not provide any information to the father or to law enforcement. *Simply maintaining confidentiality leaves the stepmother at risk.*
   c. **Incorrect.** Not provide any information to the father, and attempt to contact the client. *Contacting the client is likely a good idea, though law enforcement should be contacted first in order to protect the victim.*
   d. **Incorrect.** Not provide any information to the father, and attempt to send medical personnel to the stepmother's house. *Medical personnel may be able to assess the client on scene, but would not be equipped to prevent a violent act.*

Since all four responses include not providing information to the father, we look to the other components of each option to determine which is correct.

Practice Test Answers and Rationales

63. A couple is receiving services together by court order, after an incident of intimate partner violence led to their children being temporarily removed from the home. Though the couple is making progress on co-parenting and conflict management in therapy, they have chosen to divorce. The court orders the CSW to provide a copy of the treatment record, and the CSW is uncomfortable disclosing to the court that he diagnosed one partner with Bipolar Disorder. The CSW should:

a. **Incorrect.** Assert privilege on behalf of the clients. *Asserting privilege might still be worthwhile if the request for records came from the private attorney for one member of the couple; the court could then make a determination as to whether privilege applies. In this case, however, the CSW has already received an order from the court and is obligated to follow it.*
b. **Incorrect.** Contact the clients to determine their wishes. *Contacting the clients to determine their wishes could result in failing to obey a court order.*
c. **CORRECT.** Provide the court a copy of the treatment record. *Therapy is being provided by court order, which is an exception to privilege, and the court has specifically ordered records.*
d. **Incorrect.** Deny the court's request. *This would represent failure to comply with a court order.*

Preparing for the California Clinical Social Work Law & Ethics Exam

64. A CSW is running a therapy group for adults abused as children. Given the sensitive nature of the group, the CSW wants to begin with a discussion about privacy. Group members ask the CSW whether they can share information they learn in the group with their significant others at home. The most appropriate course of action would be for the CSW to:

a. **Incorrect.** Remind group members of their legal obligation to keep information confidential. *See rationale below.*
b. **Incorrect.** Discuss with the group why privacy is important to the success of the group process. *See rationale below.*
c. **Incorrect.** Remind group members of their ethical obligation to keep information confidential. *See rationale below.*
d. **CORRECT.** Discuss with the group what they believe the appropriate rules should be around such disclosures, as well as the consequences for violations of those rules. *See rationale below.*

The correct answer is D. Group members do not have legal or ethical obligations particular to being a client (A and C). Clear guidelines are needed, but the group can come up with their preferred guidelines with the therapist's guidance. Simply discussing why privacy is important (B) would not answer the group members' question about whether sharing information in a limited context with a trusted partner would be allowed.

Practice Test Answers and Rationales

65. A CSW is consulting with the physician who sent a young couple to the CSW for couple therapy. Both partners in the couple are struggling with symptoms of anxiety. The physician provides the CSW with useful information on the couple's medications and their possible side effects. The CSW offers the physician useful information on the progression of the couple's symptoms. Toward the end of the conversation, the physician asks whether the older partner in the couple is "still wearing that same brown sweater twice a week." The CSW should:

   a. **Incorrect.** Answer the question. *Even without a release, the CSW could answer questions directly related to diagnosis or treatment planning; however, since this question does not appear to fall in either category, it falls outside of that allowance in HIPAA.*
   b. **CORRECT.** Politely decline to answer the question, as it is not relevant to the consultation. *When taking part in a consultation, a CSW only provides information relevant to the purposes of that consultation.*
   c. **Incorrect.** Request a release from both partners to provide this type of information. *While the CSW could get a release from the clients allowing the CSW to discuss whatever the clients want the CSW to discuss, this does not change the CSW's ethical responsibilities around consultations, which include refusing to share information that is not relevant to the reason for the consult.*
   d. **Incorrect.** Gently scold the physician for asking a question outside of their scope of practice. *Scolding the physician is not the CSW's proper role; the physician may have reasons for asking the question that relate to the partner's physical symptoms.*

66. After a family session where a family's 15-year-old daughter believed the CSW sided with the mother instead of the daughter, the daughter comes to the next session wearing earbuds she refuses to take out, and demanding an apology from the CSW. The CSW should:

   a. **CORRECT.** Consider whether the daughter is correct, and if appropriate, offer an apology. *See rationale below.*
   b. **Incorrect.** Side with the mother again, reinforcing the appropriate power hierarchy in the family. *See rationale below.*
   c. **Incorrect.** Refuse to go on with therapy until the 15-year-old removes her earbuds. *See rationale below.*
   d. **Incorrect.** Demand an apology from the 15-year-old. *See rationale below.*

The correct answer is A. Remember that this test is asking about your *legal and ethical responsibilities,* not your clinical skills. (Those will be tested in the Clinical Exam.) This question is about preserving the therapeutic relationship with each individual client in a family system. That may mean offering an apology to a client who feels wronged. There may be clinical reasons in support of the other response choices, but only option A addresses the need to manage conflicts that can arise when working with more than one family member in the room.

Practice Test Answers and Rationales

67. A CSW has a client who lives on a boat three months of the year, as a commercial fisherman. During that time, he comes back to shore one day a week, and sees the CSW on that day. The client is relatively poor, and asks the CSW whether he can pay for services in fresh salmon. The client says he may need to discontinue treatment otherwise. The CSW frequently eats salmon, and so is familiar with the fair market value of the fish. Which of the following statements of the CSW's responsibilities is correct?

  a. **Incorrect.** The CSW should provide services pro bono, rather than accepting payment in fish. *Reducing fees is an acceptable resolution to the dilemma, but this response uses the word "should," suggesting that this solution is better than bartering. The carve-out in the ethics code for bartering appears to be made for precisely this type of situation.*
  b. **CORRECT.** If the CSW chooses to go ahead with the barter agreement, the value of the fish should approximate the fee generally charged for therapy, and there should be a clear contract. *While CSWs ordinarily do not accept goods or services as payment, in limited circumstances it can be acceptable. In this case, the client has specifically requested the barter arrangement, a fair value for the salmon can be easily determined, and there does not appear to be any distortion to the professional relationship that would occur. As the alternative is discontinuation of treatment, it would be ethically appropriate to at least consider the barter arrangement.*
  c. **Incorrect.** The CSW should refer the client to a low-fee or no-fee clinic rather than accepting salmon as payment. *Referring out is an acceptable resolution to the dilemma, but this option uses the word "should," suggesting that this solution is better than bartering. The carve-out in the ethics codes for bartering appear to be made for precisely this type of situation.*
  d. **Incorrect.** The CSW should consider whether other clients would also want to pay for therapy through the products they make or services they provide. *Whether a barter agreement would be appropriate for another client is not relevant to the consideration of appropriateness for this specific client.*

68. A CSW suffers a serious illness, and a colleague steps in to take over the CSW's ongoing clients until the CSW can return to practice. The CSW agrees to continue handling billing and to review the colleague's session notes to keep up with what is happening while she is recovering. Some of the CSW's ongoing clients pay for sessions through their health insurance. However, the colleague (who is also a licensed CSW in private practice) is not on any insurance panels. The CSW should:

   a. **Incorrect.** Continue to submit insurance billing listing herself as the treatment provider. *This would be a misrepresentation and may be considered insurance fraud.*
   b. **Incorrect.** Continue to submit insurance billing listing the colleague as the treatment provider and herself as the supervisor. *Because the colleague is taking over treatment, the colleague is indeed the treatment provider. Listing herself as the supervisor, however, is problematic as the colleague is apparently neither employed nor supervised by the CSW. This would be a misrepresentation and may be considered insurance fraud.*
   c. **CORRECT.** Either directly or through the colleague, inform clients of the difference in panel status and arrange alternate payment or referrals as needed.
   d. **Incorrect.** Defer to the colleague to negotiate fees independently, and otherwise presume that the CSW's typical business practices will be followed. *Each of these issues help establish why a professional will is so important. It should clarify whether the colleague can change client fees, and what business practices the CSW expects the colleague to follow. It is not safe to simply presume that the colleague's business practices will be the same as the CSW's.*

Practice Test Answers and Rationales

69. A CSW working with an adolescent client encourages one of the client's teachers to attend sessions that will focus on the adolescent's behavior in school. While the teacher's presence is at first helpful, the teacher asks to continue coming to the sessions, and it is clear to the CSW that the client is finding the teacher's presence gradually more intrusive and uncomfortable. The CSW should:

a. **CORRECT.** Clarify the teacher's role in treatment, and ask the client whether they would like to continue having the teacher in session. *When third parties are brought into treatment, that does not mean that the presence of these third parties is permanent or unmanageable. Clarifying roles on an ongoing basis in helpful and expected. Permission for third parties to be involved in therapy can be revoked in many circumstances.*
b. **Incorrect.** Ask the client whether they would like to continue having the teacher in session, and remind the teacher of the limits to confidentiality. *Reminding the teacher of the limits of confidentiality may or may not alleviate the client's concern about the teacher's presence.*
c. **Incorrect.** Ask the client to contact the school and request that the teacher be removed from the therapy sessions. *Having the client contact the school about the teacher's presence in therapy places an undue burden of responsibility on both the client and the school; if the client wants the teacher removed and the therapist believes the teacher's presence is harmful, the therapist should take responsibility for ensuring that the teacher is removed.*
d. **Incorrect.** Remind the client of the goals of therapy and the reasons for the teacher's presence in session. *Reminding the adolescent of the goals of treatment may or may not alleviate the client's concern about the teacher's presence.*

Preparing for the California Clinical Social Work Law & Ethics Exam

70. An older woman who has been seeing a CSW for seven months storms out of session after her therapist started the session some 30 minutes late. The CSW attempted to explain that another client had been in crisis, but the woman cut off the CSW, saying that the delay was disrespectful of her time. A few days later the client calls the CSW saying she will not come back for future sessions and requesting a copy of the treatment record be sent to her. The CSW should:

a. **Incorrect.** Insist that the client come in for an additional session to discuss her hurt feelings, and provide a copy of the treatment record. *The client cannot be forced to come back in, and making the discussion about the client's hurt feelings suggests that the client is to blame for feeling hurt. This is not likely to improve the fractured therapeutic relationship.*
b. **CORRECT.** Apologize for the delay, offer to discuss it further, provide options for other treatment providers, and provide a copy of the treatment record. *When treatment is terminated, even if the termination is conflictual, CSWs are obligated to provide additional treatment options for continuity of care, and this response option includes this key step.*
c. **Incorrect.** Provide a copy of the treatment record, and consider whether the client's display was simply a way of resolving cognitive dissonance about the need to end treatment. *Even if the client's departure was a way of resolving dissonance around leaving therapy -- a big leap from the information in the vignette -- referrals still must be provided to ensure continuity of care.*
d. **Incorrect.** Provide options for other treatment providers, and inform the client that the CSW will forward the treatment record to the new provider of the client's choosing, in order to ensure that the client does remain in therapy. *The CSW cannot hold records hostage and demand that the client continue treatment. Doing so violates the client's autonomy. The client requested that records be sent to her, so the CSW should either take steps to provide those records or establish why doing so would be harmful.*

Practice Test Answers and Rationales

71. A 14-year-old client who has consented for treatment independently is involved in a juvenile court case after being repeatedly caught stealing. The prosecuting attorney sends the CSW a subpoena requesting records of the client's therapy. The client expresses nervousness about their records being used against them in court. The CSW should:

   a. **Incorrect.** Contact the parents to determine their wishes, and respond to the subpoena accordingly. *Minors generally hold their own privilege, so it would not make sense to suddenly get the parents involved for this decision.*
   b. **Incorrect.** Use the CSW's clinical judgment to determine whether releasing the records would be beneficial to the minor, and respond to the subpoena accordingly. *The safe default position for the therapist is to assert privilege, and it is outside of the CSW's scope to determine whether a release of records would benefit the minor in a court proceeding. Such a determination requires legal expertise, not clinical judgment.*
   c. **CORRECT.** Assert privilege on behalf of the minor. *While minors typically hold their own privilege, they may not be able to waive it on their own. This is a decision the court would likely be involved in. Asserting privilege is a safe default position until a judge rules on whether privilege applies.*
   d. **Incorrect.** Assert privilege on behalf of the parents. *Minors generally hold their own privilege, so it would not make sense to assert privilege on behalf of parents who are not involved in the therapy.*

72. A CSW who has been in private practice for five years decides to raise her fees. Which of the following is true?

   a. **Incorrect.** The CSW may raise fees for new clients going forward, but cannot change fees for ongoing clients. *There are no rules against changing fees for ongoing clients, so long as those clients are given adequate notice and the increase is not exploitive in nature.*
   b. **Incorrect.** The CSW must provide at least 90 days' notice to all clients for any changes in fees. *While adequate notice of fee changes must be given to ongoing clients, that term is not further defined in state law or professional ethical codes. It may make sense to provide less notice for small fee changes, and more notice for more significant changes.*
   c. **Incorrect.** The CSW cannot raise fees for existing clients more than 50% in one year. *While fee increases cannot be exploitive in nature, there is no set definition for how much of a fee increase is too much. A client paying $5 per session may be able to afford a fee change to $20, even as that is a 300% increase.*
   d. **CORRECT.** The CSW may raise fees for both new and ongoing clients, if she provides adequate notice to existing clients.

Practice Test Answers and Rationales

73. A CSW is concluding short-term treatment with a casting director for a production company that is interested in developing reality television shows about therapists. The client asks whether the CSW might be willing to be considered for one of the company's shows that will be casting in a few months. The client would not be involved in the casting decision, and would not inform others at the company that he had been in therapy with the CSW. The CSW should:

a. **Incorrect.** Politely refuse the offer, as the casting decision would be made less than two years after the conclusion of therapy. *The "two year rule" in state law specifically applies to sexual relationships.*
b. **Incorrect.** Politely refuse the offer, as it would be a prohibited dual relationship. *While non-sexual dual relationships with former clients can be problematic unless an appropriate amount of time has passed, given that this treatment was short-term and the casting process would not happen for a few months, the time is enough that we could not say the possibility is absolutely prohibited.*
c. **CORRECT.** Consider the offer and inquire as to what the client's ongoing role in the show would be. *It would be appropriate to assess whether the client's ongoing role in the show might be impacted by the pre-existing therapy relationship.*
d. **Incorrect.** Consider the offer under the condition that the client disclose the therapeutic relationship. *It would not be appropriate to force the client to disclose his experience in therapy. This would represent the therapist serving their own needs rather than the needs of the client.*

74. A family tells their therapist that they keep their 5-year-old son, who is not yet in school, locked in a small room for about 20 hours of each day for his own protection. The parents report that the son has severe birth defects and sensory processing difficulties, and cannot manage social situations or significant stimulus. The parents worry that their efforts to protect him are only worsening his developmental struggles, but see no other choice. The school-age children in the family describe the son jokingly as "the monster in the closet." The therapist should:

   a. **Incorrect.** Discuss why the family describes the child as a "monster." *Simply discussing the family's description of the child, while perhaps clinically useful, does not directly address the child's suffering.*
   b. **CORRECT.** Report suspected child abuse. *Remember that the purpose of reporting is not to be punitive toward struggling families; it is to protect vulnerable populations. In this case, reporting may help connect the family with needed support services. Children with developmental delays are at added risk for abuse, and the parents' behavior likely qualifies as unjustifiable cruelty.*
   c. **Incorrect.** Ask the parents to bring the child to the next session for the CSW to assess his physical development. *It would be outside of the CSW's scope of practice to assess the boy's physical development.*
   d. **Incorrect.** Assess the parental relationship. *Simply assessing the parental relationship, while perhaps clinically useful, does not directly address the child's suffering.*

Practice Test Answers and Rationales

75. A CSW advertises her solo private practice on a professionally-designed web site. The site uses stock photography of a modern, spacious office building, and a group of seasoned professionals holding clipboards. The CSW hopes the design of the web site and the photography it includes will bring an air of professionalism and sophistication to her practice, which she attempts to carry forward in her professional demeanor. Her web site:

    a. **CORRECT.** Is likely to mislead prospective clients into believing she is part of a successful group practice. *Prospective clients can be misled by photos as well as text.*
    b. **Incorrect.** Is not expected to be a fully factual representation of her practice. *Advertisements for CSWs are required to be truthful and not misleading; an ad can be misleading even if just one part of it is misleading.*
    c. **Incorrect.** Is acceptable so long as the text on the site is accurate. *Limiting accuracy to just the text of a site does not make it acceptable. The ad overall should be clear and not misleading.*
    d. **Incorrect.** Can be effectively balanced by full disclosure at the first session that she is in individual practice. *Trying to justify a misleading ad by correcting the information at a first meeting would leave the door open to all kinds of deceptive marketing tactics among therapists.*

Appendix:
Exam Plan with Index

Board of Behavioral Sciences
Clinical Social Worker
California Law and Ethics Examination Outline

This document provides detailed information about the CSW California Law and Ethics Examination, including a description of each content area, subarea and the associated task and knowledge statements.

Each question in the examination is linked to this content.

Note: The exam outline, including all task and knowledge statements, comes from the BBS outline published online. Page numbers in the following charts refer to where the relevant information can be found within this text.

Breakdown of exam content

Content Area	Percentage
I. Law	*40%*
A. Confidentiality, Privilege, and Consent	14%
B. Limits to Confidentiality/ Mandated Reporting	16%
C. Legal Standards for Professional Practice	10%
II. Ethics	*60%*
A. Professional Competence and Preventing Harm	18%
B. Therapeutic Relationship	27%
C. Business Practices and Policies	15%

I. Law (40%)

This area assesses the candidate's ability to identify and apply legal mandates to clinical social work practice.

IA. Confidentiality, Privilege, and Consent (14%)

Task Statement	Knowledge Statement	Page
T1. Comply with legal requirements regarding the maintenance/dissemination of confidential information to protect the client's privacy.	K1. Knowledge of laws regarding confidential communications within the therapeutic relationship.	57
	K2. Knowledge of laws regarding the disclosure of confidential information to other individuals, professionals, agencies, or authorities.	57
T2. Identify holder of privilege by evaluating client's age, legal status, and/or content of therapy to determine requirements for providing therapeutic services.	K3. Knowledge of laws regarding holder of privilege.	69
	K4. Knowledge of laws regarding privileged communication.	70
T3. Comply with legal requirements regarding the disclosure of privileged information to protect client's privacy in judicial/legal matters.	K4. Knowledge of laws regarding privileged communication.	70
	K5. Knowledge of laws regarding the release of privileged information.	70
	K6. Knowledge of legal requirements for responding to subpoenas and court orders.	70

Appendix: Exam Plan with Index

Task Statement	Knowledge Statement	Page
T4. Comply with legal requirements regarding providing therapeutic services to minor clients.	K1. Knowledge of laws regarding confidential communications within the therapeutic relationship. K2. Knowledge of laws regarding the disclosure of confidential information to other individuals, professionals, agencies, or authorities. K3. Knowledge of laws regarding holder of privilege. K4. Knowledge of laws regarding privileged communication. K7. Knowledge of legal criteria and requirements for providing therapeutic services to minors.	57 57 69 70 50
T5. Maintain client records by adhering to legal requirements regarding documentation, storage, and disposal to protect the client's privacy and/or the therapeutic process.	K8. Knowledge of laws regarding documentation of therapeutic services. K9. Knowledge of laws pertaining to the maintenance/disposal of client records.	51 52
T6. Respond to requests for records by adhering to applicable laws and regulations to protect client's rights and/or safety.	K10. Knowledge of laws pertaining to client's access to treatment records. K11. Knowledge of laws pertaining to the release of client records to other individuals, professionals, or third parties.	53 53
T7. Provide services via information and communication technologies by complying with "telehealth" regulations.	K12. Knowledge of laws regarding the consent to and delivery of services via information and communication technologies.	54, 75
T8. Comply with the Health Information Portability and Accountability Act (HIPAA) regulations as mandated by law.	K13. Knowledge of legal requirements of the Health Information Portability and Accountability Act (HIPAA).	54

IB. Limits to Confidentiality / Mandated Reporting (16%)

Task Statement	Knowledge Statement	Page
T9. Report known or suspected abuse, neglect, or exploitation of dependent adult client(s) to protective authorities.	K14. Knowledge of indicators of abuse, neglect, or exploitation of dependent adults.	63
	K15. Knowledge of laws pertaining to the reporting of known or suspected incidents of abuse, neglect, or exploitation of dependent adults.	62
T10. Report known or suspected abuse, neglect, or exploitation of elderly client(s) to protective authorities.	K16. Knowledge of indicators of abuse, neglect, or exploitation of elderly clients.	63
	K17. Knowledge of laws pertaining to the reporting of known or suspected incidents of abuse, neglect, or exploitation of elderly clients.	62
T11. Report known or suspected abuse or neglect of a child or adolescent to protective authorities.	K18. Knowledge of indicators of abuse/neglect of children and adolescents.	60
	K19. Knowledge of laws pertaining to the reporting of known or suspected incidents of abuse/neglect of children and adolescents.	58
T12. Comply with legal requirements regarding breaking confidentiality to protect the client in the presence of indictors of danger to self/others and/or grave disability.	K20. Knowledge of symptoms of mental impairment that may indicate the need for involuntary hospitalization.	66
	K21. Knowledge of protocols for initiating involuntary hospitalization.	65
	K22. Knowledge of laws regarding confidentiality in situations of client danger to self or others.	65

Appendix: Exam Plan with Index

Task Statement	Knowledge Statement	Page
T13. Comply with legal requirements to report and protect when client expresses intent to cause harm to people or property.	K23. Knowledge of methods/criteria for identifying situations where client poses a danger to others.	66
	K24. Knowledge of laws pertaining to duty to protect when client indicates intent to cause harm.	67
	K25. Knowledge of situations/conditions that constitute reasonable indicators of client's intent to cause harm.	67
T14. Comply with legal requirements regarding privilege exceptions in client litigation or in response to breach of duty accusations.	K26. Knowledge of laws regarding privilege exceptions in litigation involving client's mental or emotional condition as raised by the client or client's representative.	71
	K27. Knowledge of laws regarding privilege exceptions where client alleges breach of duty.	71
T15. Comply with legal requirements regarding privilege exceptions in court-appointed and/or defendant-requested evaluation/therapy.	K28. Knowledge of laws regarding privilege exceptions in court-appointed evaluation or therapy.	71
	K29. Knowledge of laws pertaining to privilege exceptions in defendant-requested evaluation or therapy.	71
T16. Comply with legal requirements regarding reporting instances of crime perpetrated against minor clients.	K30. Knowledge of laws pertaining to the reporting of crimes perpetrated against a minor.	71
	K31. Knowledge of laws regarding privilege exceptions in crime or tort involving minors.	71

285

IC. Legal Standards for Professional Practice (10%)

Task Statement	Knowledge Statement	Page
T17. Comply with laws regarding sexual contact, conduct, and relations between therapist and client to prevent harm to the client and/or the therapeutic relationship.	K32. Knowledge of laws regarding sexual conduct between therapist and client.	100
	K33. Knowledge of legal requirements for providing client with the brochure *Professional Therapy Never Includes Sex*.	100
T18. Comply with legal parameters regarding scope of practice.	K34. Knowledge of laws that define the scope of clinical practice.	35
T19. Comply with legal parameters regarding professional conduct.	K35. Knowledge of laws that define professional conduct for licensed practitioners.	106
T20. Disclose fee structure prior to initiating therapeutic services.	K36. Knowledge of laws regarding disclosures required prior to initiating therapeutic services.	51
T21. Comply with legal regulations regarding providing treatment when interacting with third-party payers.	K37. Knowledge of laws and regulations regarding third-party reimbursement.	91
	K38. Knowledge of parity laws regarding the provision of mental health services.	92
T22. Comply with laws regarding advertisement of services and professional qualifications.	K39. Knowledge of laws regarding advertisement and dissemination of information of professional qualifications, education, and professional affiliations.	93
T23. Comply with laws pertaining to the payment or acceptance of money or other consideration for referrals.	K40. Knowledge of legal requirements regarding payment or acceptance of money or other considerations for referral of services.	90

Appendix: Exam Plan with Index

II. Ethics (60%)

This area assesses the candidate's ability to identify and apply ethical standards for professional conduct.

IIA. Professional Competence and Preventing Harm (18%)

Task Statement	Knowledge Statement	Page
T24. Consult with other professionals and/or seek additional education, training, and/or supervision to address therapeutic issues that arise outside therapist's scope of competence.	K41. Knowledge of limitations of professional experience, education, and training to determine issues outside scope of competence.	79
	K42. Knowledge of situations that indicate a need for consultation with colleagues or other professionals.	79
	K43. Knowledge of ethical standards regarding the protection of client rights when engaging in consultation/collaboration with other professionals.	80
	K44. Knowledge of ethical methods of developing additional areas of practice or expanding competence.	80
	K45. Knowledge of the ethical responsibility to remain current on developments in the profession.	80
T25. Consult with other professionals to address questions regarding ethical obligations or practice responsibilities that arise during treatment.	K42. Knowledge of situations that indicate a need for consultation with colleagues or other professionals.	79
	K43. Knowledge of ethical standards regarding the protection of client rights when engaging in consultation/collaboration with other professionals.	80

Task Statement	Knowledge Statement	Page
T26. Evaluate therapist's own mental, emotional, or physical problems/impairments to determine impact on ability to provide competent therapeutic services.	K42. Knowledge of situations that indicate a need for consultation with colleagues or other professionals.	79
	K46. Knowledge of problems/impairments that interfere with the process of providing therapeutic services.	36
	K47. Knowledge of referrals and resources to assist in meeting the needs of clients.	36
	K48. Knowledge of methods to facilitate transfer when referrals to other professionals are made.	36
T27. Provide referral(s) to qualified professionals when adjunctive/alternate treatment would benefit the client.	K41. Knowledge of limitations of professional experience, education, and training to determine issues outside scope of competence.	79
	K43. Knowledge of ethical standards regarding the protection of client rights when engaging in consultation/collaboration with other professionals.	41
	K47. Knowledge of referrals and resources to assist in meeting the needs of clients.	36
	K48. Knowledge of methods to facilitate transfer when referrals to other professionals are made.	36
	K49. Knowledge of methods for collaborating with client to determine if referral(s) or other resources are clinically indicated.	84
T28. Manage therapist's personal values, attitudes, and/or beliefs to prevent interference with effective provision of therapeutic services and/or the therapeutic relationship.	K50. Knowledge of the potential impact of therapist's personal values, attitudes, and/or beliefs on the therapeutic relationship.	37
	K51. Knowledge of methods for managing the impact of therapist's personal values, attitudes, and/or beliefs on the client or the therapeutic relationship.	37

Appendix: Exam Plan with Index

Task Statement	Knowledge Statement	Page
T29. Evaluate potential conflict of interest situations to determine the impact on the client or the therapeutic process.	K52. Knowledge of conditions/situations that could potentially exploit or cause harm to the client.	97
	K53. Knowledge of methods for managing boundaries and/or professional relationships with the client.	98
	K54. Knowledge of ethical standards regarding protecting the client's wellbeing in potential conflict of interest situations.	98
T30. Maintain professional boundaries with client to prevent situations or relationships that adversely impact the provision of therapeutic services.	K52. Knowledge of conditions/situations that could potentially exploit or cause harm to the client.	97
	K53. Knowledge of methods for managing boundaries and/or professional relationships with the client.	98
	K55. Knowledge of relationships that can be potentially detrimental to the client and/or therapeutic relationship.	99
	K56. Knowledge of methods to prevent impairment to clinical judgment and/or harm to the client in situations where multiple relationships are unavoidable.	99
T31. Adhere to ethical guidelines regarding sexual activity or contact with prospective, current, or former clients and/or those with whom the client has a personal relationship to avoid causing harm or exploitation of the client.	K57. Knowledge of the potential for client harm or exploitation associated with sexual activity or contact between therapist and client.	99
	K58. Knowledge of ethical standards regarding engaging in sexual activity or contact with client and/or others with whom the client has/had a personal relationship.	100
	K59. Knowledge of ethical standards regarding entering into a therapeutic relationship with former sexual partners.	100

IIB. Therapeutic Relationship/Services (27%)

Task Statement	Knowledge Statement	Page
T32. Obtain informed consent by providing client with information regarding the therapeutic process and the treatment process to facilitate client's ability to make decisions.	K60. Knowledge of the ethical responsibility to provide client with information regarding the therapeutic process.	47
	K61. Knowledge of disclosures that facilitate client's ability to make informed decisions regarding treatment.	47
	K62. Knowledge of client's right to self-determination in making decisions regarding therapeutic services received.	38, 48
	K63. Knowledge of methods for communicating information pertaining to informed consent in a manner consistent with developmental and cultural factors.	48
	K64. Knowledge of the right and responsibility of legal guardian/representative to make decisions on behalf of clients unable to make informed decisions.	50
	K65. Knowledge of methods for protecting client's welfare when client is unable to provide voluntary consent.	49
T33. Evaluate for current relationships with other service providers to determine impact of entering into a relationship with a new service provider.	K66. Knowledge of the effects of concurrent mental health treatments on the provision of therapeutic services.	41
	K67. Knowledge of methods for establishing collaborative professional relationships to improve the welfare of the client.	40
	K68. Knowledge of ethical standards regarding the protection of client rights when engaging in consultation/collaboration with other professionals.	41

Appendix: Exam Plan with Index

Task Statement	Knowledge Statement	Page
T34. Address confidentiality and/or therapeutic issues associated with therapist's role, treatment modality, and involvement of third parties to protect the client's rights and/or the therapeutic relationship.	K69. Knowledge of methods for identifying the "client" and the nature of relationships when providing therapeutic services to more than one person.	80
	K70. Knowledge of the impact of client unit, treatment modality, and involvement of multiple systems on confidentiality.	69
	K71. Knowledge of the factors that impact the therapeutic relationship.	85
	K72. Knowledge of methods for managing confidentiality and privacy issues when providing concurrent therapy.	42
	K73. Knowledge of methods for managing confidentiality and privacy issues when treatment involves multiple systems or third parties.	81
T35. Manage the impact of confidentiality/limits of confidentiality on the therapeutic relationship by discussing with the client issues/implications that arise during the therapeutic process.	K74. Knowledge of ethical standards regarding the management of confidentiality issues that arise in the therapeutic process.	68
	K75. Knowledge of methods for managing the impact of confidentiality issues on the therapeutic relationship.	68
T36. Manage the impact of safety and/or crisis situations by evaluating risk factors to protect the client/others.	K76. Knowledge of methods for assessing level of potential danger or harm to client or others.	66
	K77. Knowledge of ethical obligations regarding the management of safety needs.	77
	K78. Knowledge of methods and procedures for managing safety needs.	78

Preparing for the 2019 California Clinical Social Work Law & Ethics Exam

Task Statement	Knowledge Statement	Page
T37. Manage the impact of legal and ethical obligations that arise during the therapeutic process to protect the client/therapist relationship.	K79. Knowledge of the impact of legal and ethical obligations on the therapeutic relationship.	39
	K80. Knowledge of methods for protecting the best interest of the client in situations where legal and ethical obligations conflict.	39
	K81. Knowledge of methods for protecting the best interest of the client in situations where agency and ethical obligations conflict.	40
T38. Manage diversity factors in the therapeutic relationship by applying and/or gaining knowledge and awareness necessary to provide services sensitive to client needs.	K82. Knowledge of diversity factors that potentially impact the therapeutic process.	43
	K83. Knowledge of ethical standards regarding nondiscrimination.	42
	K84. Knowledge of ethical standards for providing therapeutic services congruent with client diversity.	43
	K85. Knowledge of methods to gain knowledge, awareness, sensitivity, and skills necessary for working with clients from diverse populations.	43
T39. Provide treatment that respects the client's inherent dignity and right to self-determination.	K86. Knowledge of the collaborative role between therapist and client in the therapeutic process.	38
	K87. Knowledge of the client's right to make decisions regarding therapeutic services.	38
	K88. Knowledge of methods to assist client to make decisions and clarify goals.	38
T40. Contribute to multidisciplinary team by collaborating with colleagues/other professionals to provide services that promote the wellbeing of the client.	K43. Knowledge of ethical standards regarding the protection of client rights when engaging in consultation/collaboration with other professionals.	40
	K89. Knowledge of methods for establishing collaborative professional relationships to improve welfare of the client.	40
	K90. Knowledge of ethical standards for participating as a member of an interdisciplinary team.	42

Appendix: Exam Plan with Index

Task Statement	Knowledge Statement	Page
T41. Advocate with and/or on behalf of the client by addressing barriers and/or increasing access to assist client in receiving services.	K91. Knowledge of methods for evaluating client's capacity to advocate on own behalf.	92
	K92. Knowledge of ethical standards pertaining to interacting with third-party payers.	92
	K93. Knowledge of ethical standards pertaining to interacting with other service delivery systems.	92
	K94. Knowledge of methods for enhancing client's ability to meet own needs.	92
T42. Maintain practice procedures that provide for consistent care in the event therapeutic services must be interrupted or discontinued.	K95. Knowledge of ethical considerations and conditions for interrupting or terminating therapeutic services.	82
	K96. Knowledge of referrals/resources to provide consistent care in the event therapeutic services must be interrupted or discontinued.	83
	K97. Knowledge of methods to facilitate transfer when referrals to other professionals are made.	83
T43. Terminate therapeutic services when no longer required or no longer benefits the client.	K98. Knowledge of factors and/or conditions that indicate client is ready for termination of therapeutic services.	84
	K99. Knowledge of factors and/or conditions that indicate client is not benefiting from treatment.	84
	K100. Knowledge of methods for managing the termination process.	84
	K101. Knowledge of methods to prevent client abandonment and/or client neglect.	85

IIC. Business Practices and Policies (15%)

Task Statement	Knowledge Statement	Page
T44. Advertise services by adhering to ethical guidelines regarding the use of accurate representations and information to promote services and/or expand practice.	K102. Knowledge of ethical guidelines regarding the use of accurate representation of qualifications and credentials in advertisements and/or solicitation of clients.	93
	K103. Knowledge of ethical guidelines pertaining to the solicitation of testimonials or statements from clients or others.	94
	K104. Knowledge of ethical guidelines regarding the recruitment of clients through employment and/or professional associations.	94
T45. Maintain client records by adhering to ethical guidelines to document services and/or protect the client's confidentiality.	K105. Knowledge of ethical guidelines regarding the documentation of therapeutic services consistent with sound clinical practice.	51
	K106. Knowledge of methods for providing reasonable protection of the confidentiality of client records.	52
	K107. Knowledge of ethical guidelines for releasing client records upon request.	53
	K108. Knowledge of methods to assist client understand/interpret information contained in therapeutic records.	53
T46. Clarify role(s) when acting in a professional capacity other than licensed clinical social worker to avoid confusion and/or inaccurate representation of qualifications.	K109. Knowledge of the ethical responsibility to clarify roles when acting in a professional capacity other than licensed clinical social worker.	102
	K110. Knowledge of ethical guidelines regarding engaging in conflicting and/or dual roles.	103

Appendix: Exam Plan with Index

Task Statement	Knowledge Statement	Page
T47. Implement policies/procedures that address ethical issues associated with the use of electronic media and technology in the course of providing services.	K111. Knowledge of the potential for harm to the client or therapeutic relationship with the use of electronic media in the therapeutic process.	77
	K112. Knowledge of ethical standards for implementing electronic media in the therapeutic process.	76
	K113. Knowledge of the limits and risks associated with electronic means of service delivery.	76
T48. Maintain fee/payment policies that are commensurate with services provided and protect the therapeutic relationship.	K114. Knowledge of methods and conditions for determining fees commensurate with professional services.	88
	K115. Knowledge of prohibited business practices/forms of remuneration for making/accepting client referrals.	90
	K116. Knowledge of the potential for client exploitation or harm that may result from bartering/exchanges for services.	88
	K117. Knowledge of ethical standards pertaining to the collection of unpaid balances.	89
	K118. Knowledge of ethical obligations regarding providing for continuation of treatment to the client.	89
	K119. Knowledge of ethical guidelines regarding the provision of therapeutic services when interacting with third-party payers.	92
	K47. Knowledge of referrals and resources to assist in meeting the needs of clients.	36

Preparing for the 2019 California Clinical Social Work Law & Ethics Exam

Task Statement	Knowledge Statement	Page
T49. Adhere to ethical guidelines regarding the acceptance of gifts and/or tokens of appreciation from clients.	K120. Knowledge of conditions/situations that may interfere with professional judgment or have a detrimental effect on the provision of therapeutic services.	90
	K121. Knowledge of ethical standards regarding the acceptance of gifts from clients.	90
T50. Adhere to ethical guidelines for protecting the welfare and dignity of research participants when conducting research related to the provision of therapeutic services.	K122. Knowledge of procedures to safeguard participants when conducting research projects.	101
	K123. Knowledge of disclosures required to inform participants of the nature and role of research projects.	101
	K124. Knowledge of client's rights regarding participation in research projects.	101
	K125. Knowledge of methods for protecting client confidentiality and data when conducting research projects.	102
T51. Address unethical or incompetent conduct of colleague by taking action to promote the welfare and interests of clients.	K126. Knowledge of conditions/situations that may impair the integrity or efficacy of the therapeutic process.	108
	K127. Knowledge of guidelines for addressing unethical or incompetent conduct of colleagues.	108
T52. Adhere to ethical guidelines for engaging in the supervisor/prelicensure practitioner relationship.	K128. Knowledge of the ethical guidelines governing the supervisor/prelicensure practitioner relationship and responsibilities.	102

Appendix: Exam Plan with Index

Notes

"NASW" stands for the National Association of Social Workers. "BBS" stands for Board of Behavioral Sciences. "BPC" stands for Business and Professions Code.

[1] California BPC section 4996.9
[2] NASW Code of Ethics, standard 2.03a
[3] NASW Code of Ethics standard 1.05(c)
[4] B. R. Benitez, "Guidelines for the treatment of minors," *The Therapist.*
[5] California BPC section 4992.3(t)
[6] M. Griffin, "On writing progress notes," *The Therapist.*
[7] By statute – California Penal Code section 11165.1(b), to be specific – this would be considered child abuse and would be a mandated report. However, the Department of Consumer Affairs (which oversees the BBS) issued a legal opinion in 2013 in response to my presentation to the BBS on the problems that result from this statutory requirement. The DCA opinion gives CSWs more latitude than the statute when it comes to reporting consensual oral sex, anal sex, or object penetration involving minors. Further efforts to clarify the law since then have failed, leaving the reporting requirements unclear. The BBS is aware of this concern, and as such is unlikely to include any test items that are related to this issue.
[8] National Children's Advocacy Center
[9] National Children's Advocacy Center
[10] American Psychological Association, *Elder abuse and neglect: In search of solutions.* National Committee for the Prevention of Elder Abuse, *What is elder abuse?* S. A. Salsbury, "Clinical brief: Recognizing, reporting, and responding to dependent adult abuse," *Topics in integrative health care: An integrative journal.*
[11] Named for its basis in law, which is California Welfare and Institutions Code section 5150
[12] A. Wellisch, "The 5150 foxtrot," *The Therapist.*
[13] D. Jensen, "Diagnosing a subpoena for validity," *The Therapist.*
[14] NASW Code of Ethics standard 1.13
[15] NASW Code of Ethics standard 1.13
[16] A. Tran, "Third party reimbursement," *The Therapist.*

[17] NASW Code of Ethics standard 4.04
[18] NASW Code of Ethics standard 1.06(c)
[19] BBS *Disciplinary Guidelines*
[20] BBS *Disciplinary Guidelines*
[21] NASW Code of Ethics standard 2.01(a)
[22] NASW Code of Ethics standard 2.09(a)
[23] NASW Code of Ethics standard 2.02 and 2.01(b)
[24] NASW Code of Ethics standard 2.09, 2.10, and 2.11